FREE TO BE

A Handbook to
Luther's Small Catechism

by
James A. Nestingen
and
Gerhard O. Forde

STUDENT BOOK

Augsburg Fortress
Minneapolis

FREE TO BE _____

Revised Edition

Based on *Free to Be*, copyright © 1975
Augsburg Publishing House.

This Student Book is accompanied by a
Teacher Guide.

Editors: Susan R. Niemi and Ann L. Rehfeldt
Designer: Judy Swanson

Scripture acknowledgments: Scripture
quotations from the Small Catechism are
from Revised Standard Version of the
Bible, copyright 1946-71 by Division of
Christian Education, National Council of
Churches, and are used by permission. All
other Scripture quotations are from New
Revised Standard Version Bible, copyright
1989 Division of Christian Education of
the National Council of the Churches of
Christ in the United States of America.
Used by permission.

Catechism quotations are from *The Small
Catechism by Martin Luther in Contem-
porary English with Lutheran Book of
Worship Texts* (1979 Edition), copyright
© 1960, 1968 by Augsburg Publishing
House, the Board of Publication of the Lutheran Church in America, and Concordia
Publishing House. Excerpts from the Smalcald Articles and the Augsburg Confession
are from *The Book of Concord: The Con-
fessions of the Evangelical Lutheran
Church,* edited and translated by Theodore
G. Tappert, copyright © 1959 Fortress
Press. Material identified as *LBW* is reprint-
ed from *Lutheran Book of Worship,* copyright © 1978.

7 8 9

CONTENTS

THE COMMANDMENTS

1
GOD'S DECISION

God has made a decision about you. God hasn't waited to find out how sincere you are, how devout or religious you might be, or how well you understand the Bible and the Catechism. God hasn't even waited to find out if you are interested or willing to take this decision seriously. God has simply decided.

God made this decision knowing full well the kind of person you are. God knows you better than anyone else could—inside out, upside down, and backwards. God knows where you are strong and where you are weak, what you are most proud of and what you would most like to hide. Be that as it may, God's decision is made.

God comes straight out with it: "I am the Lord your God." This is the decision: God has decided to be your God. For God wants to be as close to you as your next breath, to be the one

5

who gives you confidence and value, to open a future to you in the freedom of the Word. God wants to be the one to whom you turn for whatever you need.

God has said this before, many times. God first announced this decision about you when you were baptized. "You," God said, as the pastor spoke your name, "are baptized in my name. I am your God and I will never let you go."

God has said it since your Baptism, too, speaking on the lips of those who have loved you, whether they were part of your family, a teacher, or one of your pastors. In fact, God is saying it again in these very words: "You, you the one who is reading this, I am your God. How do you like that?"

Maybe you would like to ask a different question: Who is this God, anyway?

It is the God who made you and everything that is, the God who raised Jesus of Nazareth from the dead after he had been put to death on a cross, the one whose Spirit came like a mighty wind to drive home a word that gives forgiveness and hope. It is the God who called Abraham and Sarah out of the desert, the God who sent word to Mary that she would be having a baby, the God who covered the apostle Paul's eyes with scales and then opened his mouth with a word of freedom.

Maybe you've got another question then: What's in it for me? If God has made a decision for me, what do I get out of it?

To start with, life itself. God's decision is the life of you. For God is the one who has given you your mind, body, and all your powers, who has looked after you by night and cared for you by day, giving you all you need. The God who creates is the God of life. When this God says, "I am your God," you can expect this God to give you everything you need to live.

There's more. With God's decision, you receive the freedom of forgiveness. The God who has decided for you is the God who in Christ refuses to hold your past against you, no matter what shape it has had. The God we know in Jesus is the one who takes you as you are—with your strengths, gifts, talents, and abilities, and also with your bad habits, selfishness, pride, and whatever else you might want to conceal. There are no strings on God's decision and so no strings on you, either. You're free.

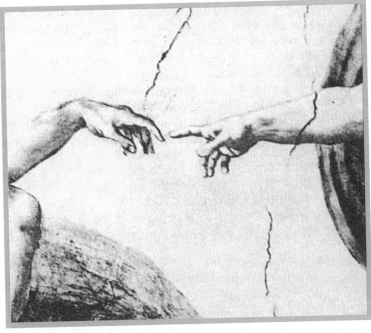

Still there's more. The God who has decided for you is the one who opened the grave the first Easter morning, the God who raises the dead. So when this God says, "I am your God," the *am* stands forever. God is, was, and always will be your God. So no grave will ever be able to hold you. In the silence of death, you will hear Jesus' voice saying, "Rise and shine. I am the Lord your God." God's decision opens your future.

Does it sound pretty good? God has decided to be your God; the God who has made this decision is the one who has created you, freed you, and assured you of the future. God's decision grants you life, forgiveness, and resurrection. You are free.

The two yous

But wait. No matter how great and gracious God's decision is, there are two yous in you and one of your yous isn't going to like this promise—not a bit. It is the you born in each of us at birth, a selfish you who wants to go it alone. It is the one in you that always wants its own way, who insists that you don't owe anything to anyone. This you is often called the *old Adam or Eve* because it is the rebellious nature passed on to us from them. It is also called the *old self* or the *old sinner* in us. It doesn't like God or God's promises because it wants its own control. The old you is going to die.

The other you is the one who makes the old you old. It is the new you, a you called out by God at your Baptism, when God first promised to be your God. It is the you who will be what God made you to be: a believer, a neighbor-lover, one who cares for the earth. Born in the water, this you lives and thrives on the word of God's promise in Christ. This you fights with the old you. As long as Christ has anything to say about it, the new you is going to live.

Does it make sense? Or is it confusing? Watch the old you and the new you fight one another a little bit and you'll see.

The old you

The old self's favorite words are *me*, *myself*, and *I*. If the old sinner in us were to have a slogan, it would be "I would rather do it myself." That is what Adam and Eve told God in the Garden of Eden, as the book of Genesis tells the story. And that is the old Adam or Eve's trademark.

This is also why the old self—the old you in you—doesn't like God's decision and promise but hates it and treats it like poison. So whenever God's promise is spoken, the old self goes to work with a vengeance.

"So what," the old you says. "God can make all the decisions God wants to make, but I'm in charge here. There's nothing I can't handle. Just leave me alone. Gods are for the weak, those who can't make it on their own."

But most of the time, the old sinner in us is a lot more subtle. Instead of hitting the promise head-on, the old sinner feints and ducks, moving and weaving to avoid getting caught. "God's decision is a great thing," it says, "but God helps those who help themselves. There must be something we can do here. We're not just puppets, after all." Before too long, the old Adam or Eve has turned God's decision into your decision—a commitment, a promise, something you have to do before God can do anything with you.

The old self can get religion, too. "God has made a decision, alright," it might say, "but not for you—you are too much of a sinner" or "you haven't tried hard enough" or "you are always in trouble in one way or another." Then the old Adam or Eve suggests its own solution: "You just do what I say," it says, "and you'll look so religious God won't be able to resist you."

But for all its talk, the old you still knows that you can't make it alone. You have to have some help of one kind or another— someone to help you out when there's trouble, something that will make you feel good about yourself, something that you can put yourself into when you would like.

This is where the old you really starts to hit its stride. The old you knows that it has no future, that it can't make it alone. So it begins to run in counterfeits—things that give a sense of power or control or security but in the end can't deliver. These are called *idols*. They are not bad in themselves. In fact, they are generally good when used properly. But they turn bad when used for the old self's purposes.

Money is an example. There's nothing wrong with money; it is a good thing, a great thing. But when the old self gets hold of a dollar, something different happens. "If only I had a lot of it," the old sinner in us will say, "then I wouldn't have to worry about a thing. Everybody would like me. I would finally get the recognition I deserve. I could buy anything I want. And if I got into trouble, money would solve anything."

When this happens, money has turned into something different. Instead of being what we earn or spend to buy what we need and a few extras, money becomes a way of buying ourselves. It might buy some happiness, for a while anyway, but when money gets mixed up with love, it turns around and starts to spend you. Every waking moment has to be arranged around getting, saving, counting, protecting, and getting more money. God, the neighbors, and the earth don't count for anything; it is just the dollar, the almighty dollar that counts.

If money won't do, the old self has a number of other idols to offer. Some might be the old fashioned kind: tin gods, statues, ancestors, the sun, moon, or stars. But most of the time the old Adam or Eve is a lot more tricky, taking the best things we have—an attractive appearance, ability in sports, good marks, a hobby, or a job—and turning them bad. When these things take hold of people's hearts, claiming fear, love, and trust, they become idols just like the statues ancient peoples worshiped.

People can be their own idols, too. That's the old self's favorite. The old sinner in us thinks we can do it all alone, all by ourselves. So it goes to work to make us fear, love, and trust our abilities and strength, manipulating within us a confidence that we can make it go without help or limit. So we get caught up in ourselves.

That's the old self's game. It is the old you in you and in each of us, a you who is bound to go it alone. God has decided to put this you to death. God won't be mocked or treated like a liar. God won't have the neighbors abused either. And God isn't going to let the earth become the old self's sewer. The old Adam or Eve will use itself to death.

The new you

God likes to be God: to create, to forgive and raise the dead, to bestow faith. So when it comes to making something new, whether within us or beyond us, God gets possessive. "Look," God says, "I've had it with the old you's mess. I know there are a lot of things you can do to help me when you're ready, but when it comes to making things right between us, you just leave that to me. I'll make a new you out of you, a you after my own heart."

So the new you—the self born in God's decision for you, drawn out of the waters of Baptism and sustained by God's promise—has a different look about it, a new look. It is the you who fears, loves, and trusts God above anything else, the you God is creating anew.

Jean-Claude Lejeune

God is to be feared; that is for sure. If the thought of meeting a great athlete, a star musician, or a well-known politician makes you nervous, think of God turning to face you. You might never recover.

But the God who raised Jesus from the dead doesn't care for intimidation. Instead, God wants to be God, to do the things that only the real God can do. So God creates, making everything from the stars and their planets to the small worlds of a flower's head or a bug's ear. God delivers, saving people from disasters, freeing us from our own clutches. God gives hope to the despairing, trust to the fearful, and confidence to the broken. There is a new you in you, a tenderhearted you whom God will move to awe, to reverence. When the word takes hold of you, bringing forth this fear, you will really be able to say, "Awesome! That's incredible! How could God do it? It is too much for words."

God is after your love, too. Sometimes God can be funny, it's true, turning our expectations on their ear, doing things we don't like or can hardly stand. That must be what it is like to be God: to do things differently. But for all of this, God is after you—especially when you're a little out of sorts with something that God had done. God loves his enemies and wants to be loved in return. So God has become lovable, in Christ, becoming a child in him and then taking on all the powers that the old sinner in us and death itself could unleash against him. There's a new you in you meant for this love. By the time God gets done with you, you won't want to say anything else but this: "Be my God, my only God. I'll never have another; you are mine."

And God wants to be trusted. God wants to be the one you call out to in a time of trouble, the one to whom you turn when things are going bad. One of the things God enjoys the most about being God, at least going by the way God behaves most of the time, is turning evil into good. God likes to do this for you, too. So when you call out and say, "God help me," God says, "I'll be right there. You just wait. By the time I get done with this, it will be better than you ever dreamed possible." There's a new you in you that God is at work on right now, a you who hollers, "God help me," in the sure and certain confidence that the good Lord is listening.

This is the new you: the you created to fear, love, and trust God above all things. It is the you who is a believer, the you God is crafting in you. If you want to do something for God, there will be plenty of opportunity. But when it comes to making this you, the new one, God says, "You just leave that to me. I'll take care of it myself."

So God speaks, announcing the decision that has been made for you. So God washes in the waters of Baptism. So God comes to the table at the Lord's Supper, gracing you once more in the Word, the eating and drinking. God has made a decision about you, to put the old you in you to its end and to bring forth the new one, the you who believes, the one in you who is identified with Christ.

Commands for the old you

The old you doesn't give up very easily. When God finishes with you, the old you will be no more and the new you—the you who fears, loves, and trusts God—will not have to fight any longer. But in the meantime, there is some struggle left. The old you isn't going to give up until it has no alternative.

So for the meantime, while the old you hangs on and the new you awaits completion, God has some commandments to hand out. They are provisional, rules for the meantime. At the same time, there is something really good about them. For in these commandments, God gives us a sense of what is most important, what matters from day to day.

In lots of ways, the Commandments are like classroom rules. If everybody came to class because of love for the teacher and the studies, there wouldn't have to be any rules. Everybody would go about learning for the joy of it. As nice as it would be, that hasn't happened yet—at least not in most classrooms. So the teachers hand down some rules: No talking during class. Raise your hand before you speak. No food in the classroom.

The Commandments work the same way. The old self knows only one rule: Everyone for herself or himself and may the winner take all. When the sinner in us gets loose, no one is safe. If God didn't keep the old you in check, the world would be even more of a mess than it is—filled with rebellion, contempt, murder, rape, and lies.

So God gives some commandments, handing them down to keep the world in order for the word of promise. The Commandments are given to keep the sinner in us under control until the word of God's decision for us takes hold and brings forth the new. God uses the Commandments to protect us and what is ours from the old self in our neighbors and in ourselves.

God uses the Commandments for another purpose, as well: to show the old self in us its true end in the promise. Here, too, the Commandments work like classroom rules. When a substitute teacher takes over, sometimes discipline is all that happens; the whole class starts to fall apart. But when classes are working the way they should work, the class stays in line and you can learn something. So God uses the Commandments to teach, to teach the old sinner in us its limits and to turn the new you toward the promise. As the promise takes hold, the Commandments quiet down; God's grace takes over.

Never one to miss an opportunity, the old self is ready to jump here. "Wait a minute," it says. "You've got that wrong. It works this way: If I do the Commandments, then God will give me the promises. I've got to have a part in this, too."

Can you see the trick? Once again, the old Adam or Eve in us comes on sounding as pious as a television preacher, concerned only about what is best for us. But there's something prickly in the piety, a thorn in the rose. If you have to do the Commandments to obtain the promise, God's decision for you isn't worth much. In fact, Christ was wasting his time. It's all up to you.

"But now just a minute, here," the old self protests. "Don't we have to do something? I mean don't we have to be sincere or at least want the promise or commit ourselves to the promise?"

It sounds good again, doesn't it? The old self wants more than anything else to hang on, even if it is just to a little tiny piece of the action. But God won't have it. "I've decided," God says. "If you want a little something to do, try the Commandments. In the meantime, I'm going to have some fun creating a new self that enjoys its freedom."

13

The whole sum

That's the First Commandment. Luther once called it the whole sum of the law and the whole sum of the gospel. It sums up all the laws and commands of God because it requires the faith of the whole person—our fears, loves and trusts, our hearts, souls, minds, and strength. It is from this commandment that all the others follow.

At the same time, the First Commandment sums up the whole gospel. It is God's promise, the announcement of the decision that God has made for you and each of us in Christ. This is the promise Paul declares in Romans 8:31 when he asks, "If God is for us, who is against us?" Because God is for us, Paul goes on to say, nothing "in all creation, will be able to separate us from the love of God in Christ Jesus our Lord" (Romans 8:39).

The First Commandment sums up the whole Catechism, too. For the Catechism is a little book of God's promises. The promises begin with this one, the most important promise of all, the one we receive in Christ's name. This promise is repeated in the Apostles' Creed, becomes the basis of our praying in the Lord's Prayer, and comes home once more in the sacraments and keys and confession.

At the same time, the Catechism is the story of death and birth: the death of the old you that fights and struggles against God, your neighbors, and the earth; the birth of the new you, born in the waters of Baptism and sustained in God's speaking. This is the new you God is making in you, the you who is a believer. As God makes you new, you will discover the freedom that God gives, the freedom that is given with the joy and certainty of God's promise.

2
MORE THAN A NAME

THE SECOND COMMANDMENT

You shall not take the name of the Lord your God in vain.

What does this mean for us?

We are to fear and love God so that we do not use his name superstitiously, or use it to curse, swear, lie, or deceive, but call on him in prayer, praise, and thanksgiving.

When God made the decision to be your God, the first thing God did was to give you a way to keep in touch: "I am the Lord, your God. This is my name."

Sometimes names are called handles. It is a pretty good description of what names do. Knowing your name, other people—your pastor, teachers, friends, and even enemies—know how to find or get hold of you. Once they have your name, they can get all kinds of other information about you, too.

The people in Bible times took names a step further, making them even better handles. The way they used names, the names said something about the person's character. The name *Jesus* means "he will save." Jesus nicknamed two of his disciples,

James and John, the Boanerges brothers—"Sons of Thunder." If you had met some Boanerges brothers in those days, you'd have expected them to be either very strong or else quick-tempered.

That's why, in Exodus 3:13-17, Moses is so interested in knowing God's name. Moses wasn't just looking for a label. He wanted a handle, a name he could take hold of to call on God when he needed help, a name that would tell him what God is like.

The name God told Moses is unlike any other: " 'I am who I am' is my name," God said (Exodus 3:14). When Moses wanted to ask God for help, he could call this name. It didn't tell Moses much about what God is like, though. All "I am" says about God is that God is, God lives, God exists.

But God told Moses a second name, as well: "Thus you shall say to the Israelites, 'The Lord, the God of your ancestors, the God of Abraham, the God of Isaac, and the God of Jacob, has sent me to you' " (Exodus 3:15). It is as if God said, "If you want to find out what I'm like, look at what I've done for your ancestors and what I do for you."

This second name must have rung all sorts of bells for Moses. "So that's who is in that burning bush," Moses might have said to himself, "the God who called Abraham and promised to make him and Sarah the father and mother of a great nation."

God has given *us* his name, too, not from burning bushes or clouded mountaintops, but in Christ. "I made your name known to them," Jesus says as he prays for his people in John 17:26. Jesus made God's name known to us not only in what he said but in what he did, through his death and resurrection.

What is God's name, then? It is

Jean-Claude Lejeune

God, God the Father who made us. It is God, God who in Christ makes us his own. It is God, God who in the Spirit calls us and makes us what we will be. Who is our God? The triune God, the one who raised Jesus from the dead.

Now that you know God's name, don't misuse it! That's what God is telling you with the Second Commandment. Once again, it's a problem of the two yous. The old you wants either to treat God's name with contempt or to use it to get its own way. To the new you, though, the you God is calling, knowing God's name means freedom: freedom to call on God as children call on a loving parent.

Making the name nothing

God's name is taken in vain whenever it is used for nothing. That is what taking it in vain means. It is used as if God were nothing and his name good for nothing.

The most obvious way of doing this is using God's name to curse. This is so common that much of the time we aren't even aware of what is being said. It is as automatic as a transmission. "God, it's cold outside." "What in God's name does she think she's doing?" "Jesus Christ, he's dumb."

When God's name is used in such a way, it becomes nothing more than a comma or an exclamation point. It is something stuffed between words to hold them apart or to give them some more emphasis; it doesn't mean anything. The name of God could hardly be treated in any cheaper way.

There are stronger ways of using God's name to curse, such as saying "God damn you" or "God damn this or that." At least when the name is used this way, the old self admits that God can do some damning. But the name is still treated as nothing—nothing more than a way to let off steam.

Propping up a lie

Another way that God's name is abused is by swearing falsely. It is using God's name to swear that we are telling the truth and then telling a lie. When this happens, God's name is nothing again—just a liar's crutch to prop up falsehoods.

The same thing happens in everyday language. "In God's name, it's the truth." "I'll swear on the Bible." "Honest to God."

17

People use God's name like this because they suspect that those they're talking to don't believe them. It's like saying, "Maybe I do lie sometimes, but when I use God's name, I'm telling the truth." The God of the promise is called upon to prop up a liar. God's name, again, is nothing.

For this reason, Jesus commands us not to swear. "Do not swear at all," he said. "Let your word be 'Yes, Yes' or 'No, No'; anything more than this comes from the evil one" (Matthew 5:34,37).

There may be times when we are required to take oaths. If you are called into court to give evidence that will help your neighbor, for instance, you may have to swear an oath. But such swearing for the benefit of our neighbors is the only appropriate kind.

A third abuse of God's name mentioned in the Catechism's explanation is using it superstitiously. Here the old self takes God's name for magic, using it in attempts to speak with the dead or other spirits, for example. Or the old you takes it as a name to be thrown in like a package of instant mix to get whatever a person wants: to sink a few free throws, to pass a test without studying, to find a fast way out of trouble.

When God's name is used magically, to do tricks or to get something for nothing, it is nothing again—nothing more than a magic word to be thrown around for the old Adam's or Eve's benefit.

The old Adam or Eve knows how to use God's name religiously, too. If it doesn't dare to abuse the name in some other way, it will teach you to use God's name to show how religious you are. When God's name is used to impress others or when we use it trying to prove to God that we deserve his gifts, we are really saying that his name, word, and promise mean nothing to us. In these ways, God's name is taken in vain as often by religious people who never curse as it is by those who use God's name to clear their throats.

Behind all of these abuses of God's name stands the old self's refusal to take God at his word. When God's decision to be our God doesn't matter, God's name doesn't count for much either. It can be taken in vain or ignored completely, good for nothing.

Freedom in the name

But now look at it again. Knowing God's name, you know the name of the one who created everything that is and will be, the name of the one who broke open the grave, the name of the one who is opening up the future to make all things new.

To know this name, God's own proper name, is a great gift. First of all, because God has promised to be your God and told you his name, you can call to God and be sure that God will hear and answer.

When God gives his name, God doesn't leave it behind the way a salesperson leaves a calling card: "Here's my name. Call me if you ever need me." God gives us his own name because God wants to hear from us, and regularly. In fact, out of God's deep love and grace, he commands us to pray, demanding that we use the name to call on him for all that we need.

It is a friendly command, like hearing your parents, pastor, or one of your friends say, "Look, I want to help you. Name what you need and I'll do all I can." Hearing such a command, we can pray, sure that God will hear our prayers. That's the first way God wants us to use the name.

Jean-Claude Lejeune

19

Knowing God's name, secondly, you can praise God. That's what you do when you receive a great gift. Because the gift is so great and because of the love that shows through it, you praise the one who gave it to you.

Praising God works the same way. It is not putting on a show, trying to work up enough goose bumps to impress yourself or someone else with how much you love God. Praise is what happens as God makes the new you, as God takes hold of you in the promise to make you one of his own. God's word and promise open your lips in praise.

Finally, knowing God's name, you know whom to thank for all the gifts you receive. That's something else that happens as you receive gifts. While you praise the gift and the one who gives it to you, you say thanks for it.

That's why God gives us both the promise and his name: to create the new you in each of us who calls upon God in prayer, praise, and thanksgiving.

God doesn't give his name lightly. It is God's personal and proper name, and it is as precious as your good name is to you. So this is the only commandment with a threat tied to it. As God gave the commandment to Moses, it reads, "You shall not make wrongful use of the name of the Lord your God, for the Lord will not acquit anyone who misuses his name" (Exodus 20:7).

God attaches such a terrible threat because the old self is always trying to make God's name nothing—using it to curse, to prop up lies, to put on a show of sham religion, as magic, and in other ways. But while God threatens the old self in you, God is at work to make you new, giving you his word again and again so that you can call to him confidently and joyfully. There is freedom in God's name—the freedom of the promise, given as God's gift.

3
THE LAST WORD

THE THIRD COMMANDMENT

Remember the Sabbath day, to keep it holy.

What does this mean for us?

We are to fear and love God so that we do not neglect his Word and the preaching of it, but regard it as holy and gladly hear and learn it.

From the moment you are called out of bed in the morning—by your parent, guardian, or an alarm clock mimicking their voices—until the moment you say good night, your day is filled with words. They pop out at you from the toothpaste tube, spill out of the radio or TV, stare at you from the cereal box, and send you off to school.

When you get there, words say hello, convey lessons to you from your books and teachers, and carry fun between you and your friends. Words follow you to the athletic field, supermarket, or wherever you go. They even invade your dreams. Words make your day.

Words make the world's day, too. Business, government, entertainment—everything depends on words. Words can be a nuisance sometimes, and they don't always do the job they should. But we'd be lost without them.

Hidden in this worldwide flood of words is one word that stands apart. It hits the ear and vibrates the eardrum just like any other word. But it is different. It is the word of the God of the promise.

Having decided to be your God and having given you his name, God is going to speak with you. God is going to tell you his decision and keep calling out the new you that will be his.

But that's not all. God has made a decision about the whole creation, which he wants to tell you about. God is going to make a new heaven and a new earth. Just as God had the first word at creation, God is going to have the last word, to make you and all things new.

Because it is so important for us to hear this word, God sends this commandment into all of the noise of our world. "Listen," God says. "I'm going to tell you the story of Jesus. And I'm going to tell you the end of the story, too—the end of your story and the world's story, what I've got in mind for you and my creation."

The new day coming

That is the purpose of the Third Commandment. God uses it to clear some time for the promise. This time also becomes a time when we can rest while we await God's new day.

God's word is "living and active, sharper than any two-edged sword," as Hebrews says (4:12). It is a powerhouse, bristling, snapping, and teeming with energy and life. When God speaks, the word goes right to work.

With the word, God made the world. By the word, Jesus healed the sick, drove out the demons, made the deaf hear, the mute talk, the blind see. And it's with the word, too, that God is making not only a new you but a brand new world. That's the goal God has set for everything that was made: to make all things new.

The promise of God's new creation coming is written all over the New Testament. When Jesus came out of the wilderness preaching and teaching, the promise of God's kingdom was the first word on his lips: "The time is fulfilled, and the kingdom of God has come near," he said. "Repent, and believe in the good news" (Mark 1:15).

It's this same promise that Paul sings of in 1 Corinthians 15:21-26 when he tells how Christ will destroy all of God's enemies, including death, the last and worst one. When that happens, the book of Revelation says, God will dwell with us, wiping away every tear. Then "death will be no more; mourning and crying and pain will be no more, for the first things have passed away" (21:4).

That's what God has in mind for the whole creation. Now the old self is hard at work in you, struggling to strangle the new you and to be done with God once and for all. Now death looms before you, rubbing its hands together saying, "Someday you'll be mine." Now the creation is filled with animosity and trouble.

But that's not the end of the story. It's not going to go on like this, one day after another, everything the same. God has decided that it won't. God's going to have the last word. God's going to write the end of the story.

When God speaks that word to bring in the new day, everything—you and the whole creation—will be made entirely new. Then all of God's enemies will be destroyed. There will be no more old Adam or Eve in you to fight and struggle against the new you God has made. There will be no more death and dying to leer at us, threatening to destroy the creation. Anything that tries to come between God and us will be destroyed.

That's how the story's going to end—not with the cold stillness of the grave but with the joy of hearing God's voice break the silence. Then we will have the final rest, the greatest rest of all, resting safe and secure with our creator. That's what we're looking forward to, the last word, the new day God has promised.

Resting in the word

It's because God wants to give us this word—the word of what has happened and will happen in Christ—that God commands us to remember the Sabbath day.

Jean-Claude Lejeune

The Sabbath is like a rest stop on a long journey. If you've been on a journey or heard about somebody else's travels, you know what rest stops are like. Sometimes they are quick, with just a few minutes to fill the tank and use the facilities. But there are longer rest stops, too, better ones where you can really rest. Then you can take some time to talk over where you've been and where you're going. And you get a chance to stretch your muscles, to rest and relax before hitting the road again.

Just as you might take time from your travels to talk over where you've been and where you're going, God takes time on the Sabbath to tell us what he's done and what our destination is going to be. God tells us of the decision that has been made for us in Christ, of his promise to be our God, to put the old Adam or Eve in us to death and make us new. And God tells us of our destination, of how Christ is going before us into the future to destroy all of his enemies and make the whole creation new.

The most important thing about the Sabbath, then, is that it is a day to hear God's word. It's not just hearing some words about God; it is God's own word, God speaking to us.

Maybe that's kind of surprising. In fact, you might even think it's preposterous—the very idea that almighty God, the maker of heaven and earth, the one who raised Jesus from the dead, would ever speak to us! But it's not just an idea; it is Christ's own promise. "For where two or three are gathered in my name, I am there among them," Jesus says (Matthew 18:20). "My sheep hear my voice," he says. "I know them, and they follow me" (John 10:27).

How does it happen, then? God speaks to us by making his word like one of our words—a word fit for the lips of pastors and teachers, farmers and pharmacists, assembly line workers and astronauts, the oldest great-grandparents and the smallest children. As your pastor and others bear witness of Christ, telling you what God has done and promises to do, God is with you, speaking to you. You have Christ's word on it—that you will hear God's word.

That makes Sunday an entirely different day. Gathering for worship isn't just getting together to hear some nice words about Jesus. It is gathering together with our neighbors to hear what Christ himself has to say to us, to hear the Word and to receive the sacraments.

There's something else that makes Sunday different, too. Just as a traveler's rest stop provides a chance to stretch muscles and relax for a while, the Sabbath provides one day each week to take it easy. We are not machines that can run day and night without ever stopping. We need some time to get out from under the load. So God commands us to take at least one day off each week, a day that is free from the everyday responsibilities of work, study, and other duties. It is a day of rest, rest in the word, a holiday in a holy day.

The ear and day plugger

You can bet that the old self isn't going to just sit still, quietly listening while God's word is spoken, though. The word is seed, sunshine, and rain for the new you and the new creation. But for the old Adam or Eve, it is a death sentence and obituary all wrapped up into one. So it squirms and fights, trying to plug your ears and your days and so deprive you of the word and the rest that goes with it.

One of the most obvious ways that the old self goes about plugging your ears and your days is by filling them with all

25

sorts of other things. It is an easy trick. You have lots of studies, and there are all sorts of interesting and fun things to be done. The old self only has to push a little bit, convincing you that there is something you really have to do or something that would really be fun, and it can rob you of your Sabbath completely.

This strategy is so successful that the old self usually doesn't have to get more clever. But it can when it has to. Sometimes the old self attacks the word with a little bit of religion. It works like this: "I read the Bible at home, when I'm alone, and I don't need the rest of that stuff." Or, "I feel so close to God in my garden, when I'm in nature"—or someplace else—"that I don't need that Sunday morning business."

If that's all there is to it—doing a little something to feel close to the Almighty—there's probably no reason to break the daily routine. But that's not the way it is. God has a word for you. Doing a little something to feel close to God is just another one of the old self's tricks designed to close ears to the word and deprive people of the company of others who will make them stronger.

Another of the old self's tricks is reserved for people who do get within earshot of the word. "Just words," the old self sniffs, "no action. All of it is just so much boring talk." Or it may try to make it seem that the word is meant for everyone but you. "God may be speaking to so and so over there," it says, "but this word certainly doesn't apply to you." Either way, the old Adam or Eve fills your ears with so many other things that you can't hear the word.

But don't you worry. God is at work to clear time so that we can rest and hear the word. And one day, sooner than we think, God is going to call the old self's number once and for all, bringing in the new day, the new creation God has promised.

That will be the end of the story that began in Jesus: God's ultimate victory, the coming of God's kingdom, "the freedom of the glory of the children of God" (Romans 8:21). This promise makes Sunday an entirely different day: a day of rest to hear the word, a rest stop on the way to God's new day.

4
THE HIGHEST OFFICE

THE FOURTH COMMANDMENT

Honor your father and your mother.

What does this mean for us?

We are to fear and love God so that we do not despise or anger our parents and others in authority, but respect, obey, love, and serve them.

God has really turned the tables. Instead of teasing you with rewards or bullying you with threats to make you swing a deal, God has come straight out and told you the whole story. In three short commandments, God has announced his decision about you in Christ, his name, and the decision he's made about the whole earth. God has said, "I'm going to be your God and make you and the whole creation new."

Now, what are you going to do in the meantime? Some people, once they hear what God has decided, think there's no point in doing anything. It doesn't seem to matter what we do anyway, they say, so why not just eat, drink, and be merry until the end.

Other people say that since God is going to write the end of the story, we'd better get busy and do some really good and pious things to prove that we are religious enough to deserve what God has in mind. That's how the old self reacts.

But what does God say? After giving you the word about your future and telling you what the end of the story is going to be, God says, "Honor your father and your mother." Then God adds a beautiful promise to this commandment: "that your days may be long in the land that the Lord your God is giving you" (Exodus 20:12). God doesn't leave us alone in the meantime but goes to work to make sure that we will enjoy long and happy lives until the new day comes.

God begins where life begins for us, in our homes. There God sets parents, guardians, and children apart for the highest offices in the creation: the offices of parent, protector, and child. Then, having protected us in our homes, God goes on with six more commandments to make sure that life and everything we need to live will be protected as long as we live.

Representatives in your house

The promise God has attached to this commandment is the tip-off to its purpose. God wants to spread an umbrella of honor over you and your family to make sure that you get a good start in life. God wants to be sure, too, that your home and community are protected and kept in order. When there is an honor among parents, authorities, and those being cared for, that's what happens—the old self is restrained and there is justice and order so that you can live a long life.

Maybe you haven't thought of *father* and *mother* as names for offices. But they are offices just as much as the offices of mayor, president, or prime minister. In fact, they are even higher offices. Parents have the highest office in the creation, because through them, God gives life. Giving life, through them, God puts parents in charge of caring for and protecting their children.

Your parents, whether you became their child through birth or adoption, received their office before you were born. God gave it to them to make sure that you would have food, clothing, a place to live, and other necessities. But that's not all. Through your parents, God has been at work to make sure that you are loved, taught, trained, and given his word and promise.

Through them, too, he's been at work to prepare you for the day when you will start out on your own.

Because the office of father and mother is so important, God has given a high office to children, too: the office of son or daughter. And just as parents and guardians have important work in their offices, God gives children a great responsibility to go with theirs. Children are to honor their parents. Does that sound like a fancy way of telling you to listen to your folks? It might, but there's more here: There is only one kind of relationship that God has set apart for something as special as honor.

You've heard that word many times before. If you get the best marks, win a contest, or earn some recognition for a project, it's an honor. As we use the word, it points to someone set apart or special.

When God uses the word, it means even more. To honor someone, as God says it, is first of all to love that person. This is where honor starts. When you love other people—your mother and father, brothers or sisters, a special friend—they become important to you. You appreciate and enjoy them, you are willing to do whatever you can for them, and you prefer them to others.

Skjold

But honoring is more than love. It includes the deepest kind of respect, respect that makes you say, "I wish I could be like him," or "If she were here, things would really be different."

A *large target*

You can see, then, how important God considers parents. In all creation, parents, guardians, and those who support their work are the only ones God commands us to honor. They are God's representatives in your house. You can see, though, what a huge job you have and what a large target the old self has to shoot at in your home.

Dale D. Gehman

The old Adam or Eve isn't just the old you in you—it's the old you in your parents, too. They're the first target. Because they have such a huge job to do, the old self has plenty of opportunities. It is easy for them to become grudging or impatient, nosy, short-tempered, hard to get along with at times, or stricter than they need to be.

What do you do when the old self causes trouble in parents? "Honor your father and your mother," the commandment answers. Two wrongs never make a right. Even when you are wronged, the best answer is always to try and make things right.

But God knows, too, that the old self can take hold of this command and use it like a club, insisting that parents be honored when it's trying to get away with the wrong. So God has put both a safety valve and a limit on his command.

The safety valve is other authorities God provides. When parents become downright mean, intolerable, or dangerous, it is the job of other authorities to help you—authorities like your teachers, your pastor, or if necessary, police officers or judges. If a difference between you and your parents becomes so important that it requires help from others, one of these people will give it. If you wonder whether the difference is worth talking to other authorities about, one of your friends can probably help you.

The one limit God has set on this commandment is simple: God is more important than parents are. That is what Jesus is talking about in Matthew 10:37: "Whoever loves father or mother more than me is not worthy of me; and whoever loves son or daughter more than me is not worthy of me." Your parents are God's representatives in your house, but they don't take God's place.

The old Adam or Eve doesn't only attack parents, however. It's the old you in you, too, and you probably don't need a long list of tricks to know how it operates.

Jim Whitmer

31

One of the old self's favorite tricks is to close children's eyes to all that their parents have done for them, so that they begin to think their parents haven't done anything or don't care. Another is making children act as if their parents and family exist to serve them and them alone, as if they were kings and queens living in a house full of servants.

There are any number of tricks that can be used to fool, anger, and annoy parents until finally they surrender. When this happens, it's not long before the house is filled with angry and shouting parents and equally angry children. The love, care, and protection that God promises to give through the home is then lost.

Because the old self attacks from both sides, the Fourth Commandment is a two-way street, running both ways to control the old you in both your parents and yourself. Paul explains it this way in Ephesians 6:1,4: "Children," he says, "obey your parents in the Lord, for this is right." Parents "do not provoke your children to anger, but bring them up in the discipline and instruction of the Lord."

When the commandment works both ways, both parents and children are helped and protected.

Parents' helpers

Maybe it sounds ridiculous to call the president or the prime minister one of your mother's and father's helpers. Usually we think of it the other way around: heads of state are the really important people, while parents are insignificant people in comparison. But that's not the way God orders things. No matter what country or kind of government, parents come first. The other authorities are to help your parents care for you.

Though your parents can provide most of the important things you need, there are some things they can't do. Most parents lack either the time or the training to give their children a full education. While all Christians can speak God's word and promise to their neighbors and children, God also sends preachers and teachers to each community. Governments are needed, too, to keep order, provide for justice, and defend the citizens.

CLEO Freelance Photo

Because these authorities help your parents, they come under the protection of the Fourth Commandment, as well. To do their jobs, such authorities—including teachers, principals, pastors, government representatives, police officers, judges, and others—need the respect and allegiance of the people they are supposed to help. Without it, they can't keep order or give the help and protection they are called to give.

The old self, of course, attacks schools, churches, and governments with as much vengeance as it attacks parents and children. As it takes hold, these authorities may become irresponsible or power hungry. When that happens, voters have the right and the responsibility to elect new officials who will do their jobs properly.

The second table

You can begin to see, now, how far God goes to make sure that each of us is taken care of properly. God wants to make sure that we can all expect to live long and happy lives while we await the new day. So, beginning with our parents, God surrounds us with people who will help to care for us in the meantime—not only authorities, but friends and neighbors.

To make sure that we can live together with friends and neighbors in peace and harmony, God has given the remaining commandments. In them, you will see how God extends a protecting hand over all that we and our neighbors need: our lives, relationships, property, names, and the hope that we need to live each day.

These commandments, from the fourth through the tenth, are called the second table of the law. In the first table, the first three commandments, God tells us about our relationship to him. Now, in the second table, God tells us about our relationship with our neighbors, commanding us to love them in every way.

These commandments aren't going to make new people out of us. That's not their purpose. But they will protect us from the old Adam or Eve and drive us to the promise. Making the new you and the new creation is a job God won't give to anyone else; that's a job God does alone.

5
THE GIFT OF LIFE

THE FIFTH COMMANDMENT

You shall not kill.

What does this mean for us?

We are to fear and love God so that we do not hurt our neighbor in any way, but help him in all his physical needs.

When car manufacturers sell cars, they usually put warranties on them—two years or so many miles or kilometers, for instance, whichever comes first. Sometimes the warranty is more, sometimes less. But once the time is up, you're on your own. If anything goes wrong, you pay the bill.

When you give a gift to someone you really care for, something different happens. You don't just give the gift and then turn your back on the person you gave it to; you want to see that person enjoy the gift. You don't turn your back on the gift, either. You make sure that it works and you see to it that no one takes it away from the person you gave it to.

That's how God gives life—not like a car manufacturer who has to worry about a profit, but like a lover who wants to take care of both the loved one and the gifts given. Because God is a lover, God doesn't give or do anything part way but goes all the way to make sure that the people and the gifts are protected.

That's what's behind this commandment. Having protected life where it begins with the Fourth Commandment, God now follows us out the door of our homes into our neighborhoods to protect our lives there.

God goes even further, not only forbidding killing—the actual act of taking another person's life—but anything that even comes close to it. These are Jesus' words: "You have heard that it was said to those of ancient times, 'You shall not murder'; and 'whoever murders shall be liable to judgment.' But I say to you that if you are angry with a brother or sister, you will be liable to judgment; and if you insult a brother or sister, you will be liable to the council; and if you say, 'You fool,' you will be liable to the hell of fire" (Matthew 5:21-22). These are hard words, but when the old self is on the loose, God's not going to take chances. Jesus puts up not only a barbed wire fence to keep the old self in, but strong mesh where it tries to sneak through.

Murder and the living death

Since life is God's gift, God won't allow anyone else to take it away. That doesn't always stop the old Adam or Eve, though. When it turns hostile, the old self can invent any number of ways to inflict pain. So there are many different kinds of killing.

Jim Whitmer

The first and most obvious one is murder. There are many kinds of murder, too: premeditated murder, in which one person deliberately sets out to kill another; passion murder, in which a person kills in a fit of anger or jealousy; and manslaughter, like a car accident, in which a person is killed through carelessness.

Another kind of killing is suicide—killing yourself. Just as God forbids other people from taking your life, God forbids you to take your own. Since life is God's gift to you, God wants you to keep it as long as possible.

There is still a third kind of killing, one that isn't quite as obvious. It is an indirect form of murder. It happens when people withhold help that could mean the difference between life and death. In car accidents, for instance, an injured person's life can depend on fast medical care. If people refuse to help when such help is needed, they can kill without ever raising a finger.

In the same way, when people who have plenty of food refuse to help those who are starving, they also become murderers. They might not deliberately set out to kill, or even know the people who are starving, but by withholding what other people need to live, they become killers just the same.

That's the barbed wire fence. God forbids taking another person's life in any way, no matter how obvious or hidden that way might be. But here's where the old self tries to crawl through. When it is afraid to kill outwardly, it tries to kill inwardly—using tricks that leave the victims alive but hurt in some way. Jesus mentions three examples: becoming angry, insulting, and calling people names.

What's wrong with anger, insults, and name-calling? They are just words; no one ever died of an insult. Maybe so, but words are powerful. If they don't kill directly, they stop just short of it. It can be awfully painful when someone becomes angry with you, when you are insulted, or called a name. If you feel weak or helpless, the words can strike like a club. That's why Jesus considers anger, insults, and name-calling forms of killing.

The same kind of thing can be accomplished without words, too. Refusing to speak to someone seems harmless. But only the dead don't communicate in some way, and only the dead are beyond talk. Refusing to speak to someone is another form of killing. It causes a living death.

That's how God protects the gift of life. God forbids us to "hurt our neighbor in any way," whether outwardly or inwardly, whether openly or in secret. For God is a lover, a lover who does everything possible to protect both the loved ones and the gifts given.

God doesn't stop here, either. When God gives us life and the gifts that go with it, God puts us to work with our gifts to help our neighbors. When that happens, the old self takes a double beating—it not only can't inflict suffering, but has to take a backseat while the new you goes to work to help others.

How do you help your neighbors? "With all of their physical needs," the explanation of the commandment says. Physical

Jim Whitmer

needs include food, clothing, shelter, and anything else that helps them maintain a full life.

Your neighbors can be helped with these needs in many ways. They are helped, for instance, through jobs your parents and you yourself do, now and in the future. God has arranged the creation so that whether we want to or not, in just about any kind of job, we end up helping others. A barber or a hairdresser helps by cutting hair; a plumber helps by running pipes full of water through people's homes; a taxi driver gives rides; a farmer grows crops needed for food; a doctor finds ways to heal; a teacher helps people learn about life, and so on.

Beyond our jobs, we help our neighbors with their physical needs by keeping our eyes open for what they need. Is your neighbor hungry? Feed him. Is she sad? Encourage her. Lonely? Visit him or her.

How far does it go?

How much help should you give? Answer that by answering another question: How much help do you need? Give your neighbors as much help as you would like in the same situation.

This commandment, then, besides being a fence, becomes a prod. God uses it not only to protect us against the old self's appetite for killing, but to drive us to Christ and our neighbors.

If the old Adam or Eve can make things tricky, as it certainly does, it can also make them complicated. Sometimes there seems to be a choice between either killing or being killed. Then there is a question: Are there some kinds of situations where it is necessary to kill?

One of these situations comes in times of war. When one country attacks another, there is killing—wholesale. What should Christians do? If we fight back, either by joining one of the armed services or by supporting the war, we wind up killing. If we don't fight back, both we ourselves and our neighbors—whether next door or across the world—may very well be killed.

Should we break the commandment and kill in order to protect ourselves and our neighbors? Or should we refuse to kill because God has forbidden it?

A clue in our neighbor

The first clue to answering these questions is in our neighbors. God has commanded us to help them in all of their needs. That includes protecting them when their lives are threatened. If your country is attacked, your neighbors are attacked. God wants you to help them. If you support the war or go off to fight, you shouldn't kill for your own benefit, but you may have to in order to protect your neighbors. Killing is never good, but at such times it may be necessary.

Other questions related to the Fifth Commandment can be at least as complicated as the question of war. One example is abortion—taking the life of an unborn child. Abortion is clearly wrong. The life of an unborn child does not belong to the mother or the father or to the child itself. It is God's. Taking life is killing.

There are some situations, though, in which abortion might be the lesser of two evils. It can happen that bearing a child might kill the mother or result in a terrible kind of living death, causing great damage to the mother, the family, or the child itself. Then it is a question like war: no matter what happens, somebody is going to be killed or forced into terrible suffering. In this kind of a situation, abortion may be the better of two extremely bad alternatives.

God not only gives life freely, but begins to protect it before we are even born. And God follows us with this protection throughout our lives, protecting us not only from murderers and other outright killers, but from the kind of living death the old self also inflicts. To protect us, God has surrounded us with neighbors and commanded them to help us in all of our physical needs. To protect them, God gives us the same commandment, commanding us not to hurt our neighbors in any way but to help them in every way.

6
SAYING NO TO SAY YES

THE SIXTH COMMANDMENT

You shall not commit adultery.

What does this mean for us?

We are to fear and love God so that in matters of sex our words and conduct are pure and honorable, and husband and wife love and respect each other.

This commandment has sometimes received a bad name as a spoilsport. It is taken as a gigantic *no* written over anything and everything connected with sex, as if it were a dump truck full of guilt, ready to drop its load on anyone caught even thinking about it.

There is a no in the commandment: "You shall not. . . ." But that isn't all there is to it. God says no to adultery—sexual relations outside of marriage—because God wants to say a much bigger yes to the companionship you have with your friends and to the marriage you may have some day.

The purpose of this commandment, then, is the same as all the others: protection. As God protects the gift of life in our homes and neighborhoods, God also wants to protect what is nearest and dearest to life itself: friendship and love. So God says no to adultery in order to protect not only you but your whole community.

When two become one

From the beginning of the creation, God has been concerned that all people have some companions or friends, that no one is left completely alone. Next to life itself, companionship is one of the best and most important gifts. God wants to make sure that we have plenty of it while we await the new day.

If you think over your friendships, or what it's like to be without friends, you can see some of what makes them so much fun and so important. To start with, friends are people you can enjoy—people you have things in common with, people who are interesting and fun to be with. But there's more to it. A friend is someone you can confide in and trust. You can talk to your friends about what troubles or angers you, confident they won't betray you. And when you need help, you can be pretty sure that your friends will give it to you.

It's not only a one-way street, though. Part of what makes friendship so enjoyable is that your friends do the same with you, confiding in you and leaning on you for help as it's needed.

There's only one kind of companionship closer than friendship. That is marriage. "From the beginning of creation," Jesus says, " 'God made them male and female.' 'For this reason a man shall leave his father and mother and be joined to his wife, and the two shall become one flesh.' So they are no longer two, but one flesh" (Mark 10:6-8).

When a man and a woman become one flesh in marriage, it has all the marks of a friendship. They enjoy one another's company, confide in one another, and depend on one another for help. But marriage goes further than friendship. It is a man and a woman giving themselves to one another completely, as lifetime partners in God's promise.

An important part of this giving is sexual. The man and the woman become one flesh in their bodies, expressing their love for one another by giving their bodies to each other.

As they become one in their bodies, husbands and wives become like one person. Though they are still two people, they are united so that they can be together without fear or

Jim Whitmer

shame, sharing all that they have—their days, months, and years; their abilities and disabilities; their gifts and needs; their whole selves.

This companionship is the first purpose of marriage. With it, God gives another gift: children. That's the second purpose of marriage. Through it, God gives life to families and new generations of people.

Marriage is both private and public. It is a private companionship, one that belongs to husbands and wives by themselves. Marriage is also public, especially as a child or children are born. The husband and wife become father and mother, taking on the offices we spoke of in relation to the Fourth Commandment.

Your community has an interest in marriage, too. For when two become one they can soon become three, or four, or more. Families provide not only the people who will keep communities going but the honor necessary for any kind of public life. Communities of people begin in marriages and families, receiving not only more people but the help and service each family gives.

Now there are some people who don't marry. Sometimes it is because they choose not to, believing that by not marrying they can make best use of the gifts and talents they have. Sometimes there are other reasons, such as not getting the right opportunity. Whatever the reason, God sees to it that no one is left completely alone, that all of us have companions. Unmarried people have their own special gifts to bring to our communities.

43

When two become three

When two become one, they can become three in another way, besides having a child. They can become three by the interference of another person from outside the marriage. That's what happens in adultery. If marriage is a circle with two halves, adultery is a triangle that breaks it.

It doesn't only happen in marriages. Sometimes two become three in friendships. Maybe that's happened to you—you've had a close friend and lost him or her to a third person. Or maybe the third corner of the triangle hasn't been a person at all but some new interest or hobby your friend has taken up. It happens both ways. Either way, the friendship is lost.

Now there's no law, in the Commandments or anywhere else, that says friendships have to last forever. That's an important part of your freedom. As you change and develop new interests, you have to be free to change your friendships, too, making new acquaintances who share your interests. God doesn't limit us to one friend apiece.

But when two become three in a marriage, it's a different story. If the old self succeeds in making the circle a triangle, all the gifts God gives in marriage are broken. That's why the commandment against adultery comes right after the commandment against killing; it is the closest thing to murder. Though no person may be killed, in adultery a marriage dies.

Adultery kills

The first thing adultery kills in a marriage is the companionship. It's like discovering that your closest friend has been telling your secrets, only a dozen times as bad. When a man gives his body to another woman, or a woman gives her body to another man, the trust and confidence they've had with their partners are broken. They can't be sure of each other anymore or be together without suspicion of some kind.

When the companionship between a husband and wife is broken, any children get caught, too. They don't get the kind of loving care and help from their parents that God gives through families. And even if they aren't left without a father or mother, they still bear the burdens of their parents' troubles.

Finally, the community is hurt by adultery. The third person in the triangle is usually a part of the community, too, and comes from a family. Then there are two families in trouble. But even if it's just one family, adultery breaks that family's gifts and causes problems for others.

That's why God forbids adultery. The old self can get some satisfaction in it, crowing about needs and fulfillment. But that pleasure rebounds to destroy the gifts God wants all of us to receive.

That's why Jesus has tightened up this commandment. "You have heard that it was said, 'You shall not commit adultery.' But I say to you," Jesus said, "that everyone who looks at a woman with lust has already committed adultery with her in his heart" (Matthew 5:27-28). With the Commandments, God puts a fence around adultery where it ends—in another person's bed. With these words, Jesus puts a fence around adultery where it begins—in the desire of the heart.

It might seem that Jesus is being too strict. Sex is exciting—it can be easy for men and women to think they can treat each other casually, as though sex were just a more involved way of shaking hands. "Just looking" doesn't seem to hurt anyone.

But that's where adultery begins—in looks, in daydreams, in casual disregard. "Just looking" isn't *just* looking, Jesus says, but adultery already. The triangle is starting to form, even if it's only in your mind.

Jesus isn't only speaking of people who are already married here. "Anyone," he says, "anyone who looks lustfully." Though you may not marry for several years or get married at all, God is already at work to protect you and the gifts he will give if and when you do marry.

It's not that God considers sex evil or nasty and wants to blind you until your wedding day. Your sexuality and the desire that goes with it are God's gifts to you. But while God gives you these gifts, God wants to make sure that you are free to change friends as you need to. So God forbids you to give your body to anyone until you have publicly declared that that's the person you want to spend your life with. In this way, God protects your freedom now and the joy of the marriage you may have in the future.

45

For a lifetime

Jesus has some strong words to say about divorce, too. "But I say to you that anyone who divorces his wife, except on the ground of unchastity, causes her to commit adultery" (Matthew 5:32).

Now again, those words seem terribly strict, especially to the old self. The old Adam or Eve always wants to serve its own ends and so would like to be free to do whatever pleases it.

But Christ wants to protect marriage as much as possible and to keep the old self in line. That's why he says this no to divorce. When you give yourself to your husband or wife, Christ wants to be sure that it is for your lifetime, that you receive all the gifts of marriage not only part-time but full-time.

Sometimes the old Adam or Eve will turn these words around and try to use them to its own advantage, though. In some families, the marriage may be so totally broken that divorce may be the only way to prevent further damage. In such cases, the old self will sometimes piously invoke Christ's words and say that divorce is impossible, just so it can do more damage. When that happens, divorce may be the best of bad alternatives.

There are some big nos in this commandment. God says no to adultery and anything that comes close to it. At the same time, though, God is saying a much bigger yes to you, doing everything possible to protect you and your marriage and commanding you to do the same.

God does something besides commanding and protecting; God forgives. When the old self succeeds in making a triangle— whether it is in adultery by looking, adultery in somebody else's bed, or a divorce—God doesn't come around to say, "I told you so." Instead God says, "I am the Lord your God," renews you in the promise, and keeps right on working to give you companions while you await the new day. That is a gift even greater than life and marriage: in Christ, God promises to be our God, a greater companion than anyone else could ever hope to be, forever.

7
A PARADE OF THIEVES

THE SEVENTH COMMANDMENT

You shall not steal.

What does this mean for us?

We are to fear and love God so that we do not take our neighbor's money or property, or get them in any dishonest way, but help him to improve and protect his property and means of making a living.

What's God doing worrying about property? In each of the other commandments, God has been protecting life in one way or another. Is property as important as life? Important enough for God to be concerned about? Why should the God of the promise bother about the change in your wallet, the clothes that hang in your closet, the plate on your table, the bicycle in your garage?

There's an easy answer: God is concerned about your property because there are some things you can't live without while you await the new day. Food and clothing, to start with. And that means money to buy them. You need a place to live and medicine when you're sick. When you go to work you need books or training, tools, and some kind of transportation. Because God knows that you need these things and others, God has forbidden anyone to take them from you unfairly.

But there's another reason for God's concern for property. All property belongs to him—every last shred of it. God made everything. So, while God protects your interests and your neighbors', God is going to protect what he's made, too.

It takes a thief

God has arranged the creation in such a way that all of us wind up trading with other people. Whether it is a candy bar, a loaf of bread, or a used car, it is the same basic rule: to get what you want, you give the other person what he or she wants.

When this trading is done fairly, everyone benefits. Take a loaf of bread, for instance. The basic ingredients in the bread started out as wheat in a farmer's field. The farmer got some benefits by selling the wheat to a co-op or a milling company. A miller, in turn, benefited by grinding the wheat into flour

Photo Agora

and selling it to a baker. The baker benefited by baking bread from the flour and selling it to a supermarket. The supermarket's owners and employees benefited by selling the bread to you. And finally, you and your family benefit by eating it.

That's the way trading is supposed to work. God has given each one of us something that our neighbors need so that by trading, all of us help one another. As God gives us these gifts, God wants to be sure that they are used properly, that there is justice for all in trades that are fair and square.

The old self has a different idea. When the old self sees something that belongs to the neighbor, it is all hands, ready to grab as much as it can get. All that matters to the old self is its own well-being. It is the old you that always wants something for nothing.

That's why God forbids stealing. In a fair trade, everyone benefits. But in stealing, only the thief profits. The neighbors are robbed of the good they are supposed to get from what God has given them. If you can manage to get out of the supermarket with that loaf of bread without paying, for instance, you'll get the loaf of bread and save the cost. But the owner of the supermarket will take a double loss, losing both the bread and the extra money it takes to replace it.

That kind of stealing—shoplifting—is easy to recognize. So are burglary and robbery, pickpocketing, purse snatching, and other open kinds of theft. But there are many other kinds of thievery that aren't so easily recognized. They don't appear to be thefts, and so they often slip by unnoticed.

One of them is dishonest trading. This happens when merchants overprice or sell shoddy, poorly made merchandise. It is not wrong to make a reasonable profit; storekeepers deserve some benefit from what they sell. But merchants who overcharge take far more profit than can rightfully be asked, and the customers go away with less than they deserve.

The same goes for shoddy merchandise. A car dealer who sells your family a poorly made car steals several times: once when you don't get what you've paid for—a good car—and after that every time the car has to be taken back for repairs that shouldn't have been needed in the first place.

The most common theft

This kind of stealing is by far the most common form of theft. There are all kinds of people who sell their services for outrageous prices just because they can get away with it. There are all kinds of other people who don't pay for the services they receive. There aren't many employees working who won't steal a few minutes from an employer when there's a chance. And there aren't many employers who lie awake nights worrying about paying their employees enough.

The parade of thieves is awfully long. At the front are burglars, robbers, shoplifters, pickpockets, and swindlers. Behind them comes a much longer line of dishonest traders and dealers. And behind them follow all of us who try to get more from our neighbors than we are willing to give in return. That makes the whole world a parade of thieves, all of us marching along as the old Adam or Eve beats the drum to convince each of us to grab as much as we can get.

God is speaking to all of us with this commandment. By forbidding stealing, God protects each of us so that we will be able to keep what we need to live until the new day.

The Creator's stewards

God has another reason for being concerned about property: it is all his. So God wants to make sure that it is used properly. Jesus tells a parable in Matthew 25:14-30 that shows how this happens. The parable is about a man who went on a trip.

Before he left, the man called in three of his servants and gave them some of his property to take care of. The first servant got five talents, about 75 years worth of wages. The second man got two talents, 30 years worth of wages. And the third servant got one talent to look after, 15 years worth of wages.

As soon as the owner left town, the first two servants went to work. They traded with their master's money, buying and selling. By the time the master returned, they had doubled his money.

The one-talent man wasn't as brave. Maybe that isn't so surprising. Being left with even a year's worth of wages to look after would be a big responsibility. So, afraid of everything that might happen to the money, the man buried it. When the master returned, the servant dug up the talent and gave it back.

As you can imagine, the master was pleased with the first two servants. As you can imagine, too, he wasn't at all pleased with the third servant.

What do you make of this parable? First of all, look at how generous and trusting the master was. He gave each of his servants a tremendous amount of money. He didn't threaten or warn them about what would happen if they lost it. "He entrusted his property to them," Jesus says.

A second hint is how the two servants used their master's money. They helped their master by getting him a return on his money. And they helped their neighbors by trading with them.

A third hint is in what the third servant did. His talent didn't do anyone any good, neither the master nor any neighbors nor the man himself.

Who is that generous?

Can you put the hints together? Who would ever be as generous as that master, or as trusting? Which master is concerned that we serve not only the master but our neighbors?

The master in the parable is like the God of the promise, isn't he? Only God is even more generous. After God has announced his decision, "I am the Lord your God," God goes to work to give us and our neighbors everything good. God makes the sun shine and the rain fall on the good and the bad alike (Matthew 5:45).

What's more, when God gives us all of these great gifts, God doesn't look over our shoulders like some anxious father or mother, afraid we won't be able to handle the gifts. God trusts us to use the things given to us to help our neighbors "improve and protect their property and means of making a living."

There is also a word of warning in this parable, though. God doesn't look over our shoulder to make sure we use wisely the property we receive. But God won't be mocked, either. That's what the third servant found out.

God doesn't give us property just for our own benefit. God gives it to us to be used for his benefit, the benefit of our neighbors, and finally for our own good. God won't stand for the old self's selfishness, greed, and hoarding.

Each day God gives us everything we need to live while we await the day when his kingdom will come. But while looking after us and our neighbors, God also looks after the whole creation so that the deal is fair and square for all concerned.

8
FENCING THE HEART

THE EIGHTH COMMANDMENT

You shall not bear false witness against your neighbor.

What does this mean for us?

We are to fear and love God so that we do not betray, slander, or lie about our neighbor, but defend him, speak well of him, and explain his actions in the kindest way.

Do you think God knows your name? It might seem impossible. You are just one person—not only one in a million, but one in billions.

But God does know your name. In fact, when God made the decision to be your God, he gave you your name. It happened when you were baptized. As the pastor spoke the word and washed you with water, God joined your name to his. "Vance William" or "Erica Louise," the pastor said, "I baptize you in the name of the Father, and of the Son, and of the Holy Spirit."

Having given you your name, God is as concerned about it as about his own. You remember how God protects his name with the Second Commandment. In this commandment, God is doing the same for yours. And God protects your name for the same reason: it is your handle. People use it to get hold of you, to speak with you and about you. A good name means freedom: the freedom to live and move and serve as you await God's new day. So God protects it.

The freedom in your name

You don't have to look far to see the differences between a good name and a bad one. Classmates who have good names with your teachers, for instance, have an easier time of it. If there is any trouble in your classroom, the teacher will usually assume that those with good names aren't to blame. And when it comes time for grades, a student with a good name will usually get the benefit of the doubt. A bad name works just the opposite.

The kind of name you have makes a big difference with your classmates, too. Whatever causes it, when people get bad names they soon learn that there are some people who won't have much to do with them. If the word gets out that they do drugs, steal, or that there's something else wrong with them, people may avoid them.

The kind of name you have, then, is awfully important. It makes a tremendous difference in how well you do at school, what kind of friends you have, and the kind of opportunities you get.

The name you get now will follow you away to a job or a college, too, in your records and recommendations. And the name you get there will follow you the rest of your life.

No wonder, then, that God is so concerned about your name. It's not only a handle. It's a key. When your name is good, there are all kinds of freedom in it. It opens doors so that you can go places and do things; people accept, respect, and appreciate you. If your name gets bad, the doors close; there are places you can't go, things you can't do, friends you can't have or keep.

There's nothing the old self wants more in both you and your neighbors than to build up a name that people respect. If you can get hold of that kind of key, it can open the doors to all kinds of other tricks.

Jeffrey High

To get this kind of name, the old Adam or Eve takes shortcuts, trying to make a name for you by dragging down the names of others around you.

The name dropper

One place the old self can do this is in law courts. When people are sued or accused of crimes, their names are at stake. If they lose, they will be fined, spend years in prison, or both. And the bad names they get will follow them for many years.

With so much at stake, the old self has good hunting in the courts. To drag down the name of another person there, all it takes is a few lies or half truths on the witness stand. The witness can claim a good name for testifying against a lawbreaker, and the victim pays the cost of it.

That is the first thing God forbids with this commandment: bearing false witness against someone in a courtroom or other places where authorities are searching for the truth. God forbids it not only to protect you and your neighbors, but to keep order in your community. Lying witnesses destroy the justice we need to live together peacefully.

But courtrooms are just the beginning. The old self can destroy names wherever people talk with one another, whether it is at school, in church or a restaurant, on the phone, or on paper. And it has a whole arsenal to hunt with. One of the old self's weapons is slander, saying something false about another person that damages the person's reputation. Another is betrayal, passing along secrets or other information someone would prefer to keep private. A third is gossip, truths, half-truths, and rumors that put other people in a bad light.

All of these weapons are easily used. They strike quietly in little comments like "that teacher isn't fair," "that girl is stuck up," or "that guy cheats." But no matter how small they seem, these comments can do terrible damage.

In fact, whole sexes and races of people have gotten bad names from small comments. Men have taken away part of the good names of women by saying that they are less able than men. People of some races have lost much of their freedom because of these kinds of attacks. Once good names are lost, the freedom that goes with them is very difficult to regain.

To protect our good names and our freedom, then, God has forbidden the old self to use any of these weapons or to do anything else that hurts somebody's name.

God goes further, too. God commands us to care for our neighbors' names. That includes defending our neighbors when others speak ill of them, finding opportunities to say good things about them, and giving them the benefit of the doubt when they do something wrong.

To the old self, this seems terribly unreasonable. As the old Adam or Eve sees it, other people's faults and failings are an opportunity to make you look a little bit better. "You might not be so good," it will say, "but at least you're not as bad as that person." And it doesn't have to be a public comment. The old self can enjoy a neighbor's faults in silence, basking in that person's difficulties like a dog or cat lying in the sun.

But as Christ makes the new you, something different happens. Because God has given you your name and cares for you, you can see to it that other people's names are cared for, too. Then it's not just a matter of keeping silent when others' names are attacked, but a matter of seeing to it that their names are kept open and the freedom in their names is protected.

Jesus takes the protection of this commandment one step further by suggesting a way to handle differences that come

Jean-Claude Lejeune

between neighbors. Because we aren't in heaven yet, there are bound to be differences. Whatever causes them, these differences are a golden opportunity for the old self. To prevent the sinner in us from using these opportunities for the worst, Jesus has laid out three steps to take care of the problems.

The first step is to speak to your neighbor. "If another sins against you," Jesus says, "go and talk to the other about it. If the other listens to you, everything will be fine" (based on Matthew 18:15). That is the last thing the old self wants to do. Instead, it tells the whole neighborhood or, if it's more timid, at least some strategically placed friends. If the old Adam or Eve speaks to the neighbor about it at all, it is only after it's gotten all of the mileage it can out of the fault.

Jesus turns it around. If your neighbor says or does something that bothers you, that person should be the first to know. Then he or she can explain or apologize. If what bothers you isn't important enough to take the risk of talking to the person who caused the problem, the best thing to do is to keep quiet about it.

Telling your neighbor about something that offends you doesn't automatically mean a change, however. So Jesus has suggested a second step. "But if you are not listened to, take one or two others along with you" (Matthew 18:16). It is at this point that the old self does something different, becoming a tattletale. After blowing it all over the neighborhood when the sinner in us finds some difference with the neighbor, it finds someone to tattle to—the teacher, the pastor, the police, or some other authority. If it can't get it's own way, it will try to use the authorities to accomplish its own purpose.

A second chance

Instead, Jesus says, give your neighbor a second chance. Take one or two other people along with you and talk to your neighbor again. That way, the neighbor has another chance to learn that you are serious about the problem and want to have it solved. If the person still won't come around, you have the benefit of some witnesses who know that you have done everything you can to take care of the problem.

The third and final step is to tell the authorities. "If the other refuses to listen to them," Jesus says, speaking of the witnesses, "tell it to the church" (based on Matthew 18:17). If your neighbor won't listen to you after you've spoken to him or her privately and then come with witnesses, there is no alternative but to make it public—not by noising the wrong all over the neighborhood, but by speaking to the authorities. If it is someone in your congregation, take it to the pastor or the council. If it is someone in your class, talk to your teacher. If it is something for the police, speak with them. One of these authorities can then take the proper steps to make sure the problem is laid to rest.

You see what great care God takes to protect our names. God not only forbids betraying, slandering, and lying about one another, but commands us to speak the truth in love, loving our neighbors enough to keep quiet about their faults unless we speak to them directly.

God is so concerned about our names because of the freedom in a good name: the freedom to live and serve well, confident of people's acceptance and respect. God will protect your name and your neighbors' names to the end, keeping the earth ready for the day when the old self—with all of its name-dropping and name-destroying—dies forever.

9
COUNTERFEIT HOPE

THE NINTH COMMANDMENT

You shall not covet your neighbor's house.

What does this mean for us?

We are to fear and love God so that we do not desire to get our neighbor's possessions by scheming, or by pretending to have a right to them, but always help him keep what is his.

THE TENTH COMMANDMENT

You shall not covet your neighbor's wife, or his manservant, or his maidservant, or his cattle, or anything that is your neighbor's.

What does this mean for us?

We are to fear and love God so that we do not tempt or coax away from our neighbor his wife or his workers, but encourage them to remain loyal.

Have you ever wished that you were someone else? Have you lain awake at night thinking about what it might be like if you were a little taller or shorter, a little stronger or faster, a little prettier or not quite so heavy—like someone else you know? Have you ever daydreamed about winning some special kind of honor? Or have you ever gone to sleep dreaming about what a difference it would make to have something special— a driver's license and a car, maybe a new stereo, some special clothes, a camera, a shortwave radio, or something else?

Dreams and daydreams are full of hope, something we can't live without. Hope is having something to look forward to, something to wait for tomorrow, the day after, and in the days to come. It is as necessary to us as life and breath, our homes, property, and names.

Having made the decision about us in Christ, God gives us all kinds of hope. God gives us hope for the new self and the new day coming, the final day when God will have the last word and bring in the kingdom. And in the meantime, God gives us hope in the promise to care for us each day, the promise to give us everything we could possibly need to live and serve and be useful.

The old self knows how important hope is, too. But since the sinner in us doesn't have a future of its own, it offers a counterfeit. The old self's false future is centered not on God's promise, but on yourself. In the place of hope, the old self offers coveting: setting your heart on someone or something that belongs to another person.

This false hope is often hidden in your daydreams and wishes. That may seem strange. There doesn't seem to be anything wrong with wishing or dreaming. It can inspire you to work hard, to go places, and to accomplish things. Dreaming is good in a lot of ways.

You know by now, though, that the old self is the master of counterfeiting and disguise. It hides itself in what looks good to have its way. That's why God has given two commandments to go after something as innocent looking as wishing.

First of all, as long as the old Adam or Eve is filling you and your neighbor with wishes for things you think you need to make your life complete, neither you nor your neighbors are safe. Secondly, the old self uses these counterfeit hopes to make a slave of you and finally to burn you out. Then there is no hope.

Fencing the wish

If you've watched the commercials on television instead of running to the refrigerator or somewhere else during the program breaks, you've already seen some good examples of how dangerous wishes can be.

Take car commercials, for example. No matter how fancy or expensive the cars may be, they can only do one thing: haul you from one place to another. Some are large, some small; some get better mileage, some worse; some are more reliable than others. But there isn't one of them that can make you any sexier, any more intelligent, any more beautiful or handsome than you already are.

You wouldn't know that from the commercials, though. Each year the car companies spend millions to convince you and your parents that buying a particular model will change your life—that it will make you more distinguished, elegant, beautiful, daring, or desirable.

That is how coveting works. The advertising is legal but underhanded, designed to make you think you have to have a certain car to be the person you want to be. The car companies covet your money and use the tricks of advertising to make you covet one of their cars.

Another example of coveting happens in friendships. There is no law that says friendships have to last forever. There is nothing illegal about a third person wanting to become a friend of one of your friends, either. But if that third person tries to come between you and your friend, using tricks and schemes to do it, there is something wrong, no matter how legal it is. Though the third person may not outwardly break any of the Commandments, the tricks the person uses can separate you from a close friend and leave you alone.

The purpose of these commandments, then, is to close up these kinds of legal loopholes. Women are not property as they were considered when the wording of the Ninth and Tenth

Commandments originated. Very few people have menservants and maidservants, and most people don't have cattle, either. But there are all kinds of tricks and schemes the old Adam or Eve can and does use to sneak through the other commandments, keeping all the appearances legal while working to deprive you of what is rightfully yours.

That's why coveting is so dangerous. When you want what belongs to your neighbors, they aren't safe. When they want what belongs to you, you aren't safe, either. Even if the desires don't turn to outright adultery, theft, or tricks, wanting something or someone who belongs to another person is the first step toward trying to take it away. When you want what belongs to others and others want what belongs to you, you can't be together without envy and suspicion.

So by forbidding coveting, God works to maintain order in our communities. When covetousness is broken, we can wait and work with our neighbors, helping one another to keep what we have, looking forward together to the day when God will bring in the new day. That is real hope, not a counterfeit that makes us envious and suspicious of our neighbors.

The bad penny comes back

Like counterfeit money, the old self's wishes don't just cause trouble for neighbors. They come back to haunt you. Only it's worse than haunting. Your wishes can make a slave of you and give you a worse enemy than you've dreamed of or met.

Take a car, for instance. Suppose the ads succeed in convincing you that if only you can get your hands on one special car, your whole life will change, that the car will make other people more interested in you, that you'll be sexier, happier, a real man or a real woman if you buy and drive it.

How would you go about getting such a car? Obviously, you couldn't steal it. If you did, you couldn't drive it around town. And the car companies aren't easily deceived. Somehow, you would have to find the money to buy it.

Then what would happen? Well, pretty soon your whole life would be devoted to getting enough money for that car. You'd make sacrifices, working after school, on Saturday, and perhaps on Sunday, saving every penny you could lay your hands on.

There would be little time for friendships, school, or fun.

If you finally got the car, it might succeed in making you the envy of your school, town, or neighborhood at first. But pretty soon you'd wonder if all those people were interested in you or your car. More than likely you'd have to show that no other car nearby was better than yours. And you'd probably worry that someone might scratch the finish or do some other kind of damage out of envy.

Besides that, you'd have as much work on your hands as ever: making money to buy fuel; washing, waxing, shining, and maintaining the car. Again there wouldn't be time for school-work, not even enough time to drive the car around, or for friends other then those who really like the car.

It might sound like an attractive kind of slavery. Having a car like that could be a lot of fun. But it would be a slavery just the same, wouldn't it? Everything would have to be organized and sacrificed for the wish—that beautiful "slave maker." That's probably why so many people who get cars like that get tired of them after a while. The wish, which started out as an innocent daydream, has made them slaves.

Cars aren't the only culprits. There are as many slave makers as there are things to covet. Athletes who covet prizes and the recognition they can bring can become blue-ribbon slaves. The same thing happens to people who covet being beautiful. They spend all kinds of time grooming to look just right. They buy only the latest fashions and worry about how they look and what others think of them. They might be beautiful, but they are as much slaves as the ones who wear chains.

Every one of the old self's counterfeit hopes promises some

kind of joy, some special recognition or honor, some special reward. And every one of them eventually falls short. The fancy car is soon outdated or it rusts and wears out. Athletes lose games and are soon forgotten. The beautiful people quickly find out that beauty isn't everything or that they aren't as beautiful as they thought.

When these hopes burn out, the old self has to run out and find other counterfeits to take their places. They burn out, too. Finally it looks as though every hope is counterfeit and we're burned out entirely, hopeless, full of despair, certain that nothing is any fun anymore.

That's the second reason God forbids coveting: to protect us from ourselves. We are our own worst enemies, suckers for just about every counterfeit hope the old self drags in front of us.

Protecting us from ourselves

So God, as a gracious and loving creator, works to protect us from ourselves by forbidding these kinds of wishes before they can get off the ground. "You shall not covet," God says. "Don't set your hearts on what belongs to your neighbors— not on the people who belong to them, not on the things that belong to them, not on the recognition, honor, or praise they can give you."

But God doesn't stop after saying no. He says no to the old you's false hopes because God is saying a much bigger yes to the new you, giving you a hope that won't fail. God has decided to be your God, to give you and all of us a hope that is real, not counterfeit. It is the hope of the promise that there is a new you, a new day coming when God will dwell with us, wiping out death, every tear, all mourning, sorrow, and pain.

God gives wishes, dreams, and hopes in the meantime, too— everything we could wish for, dream of, or hope for to help our neighbors and care for the earth. In fact, that's the only limit God sets on our wishing: that it not be at our neighbor's expense, the creation's loss, or our own. God's going to be our God, after all, right up to the day when we are raised from the dead and forever after. With that promise, God makes everything we need a gift.

10
A JEALOUS GOD

WHAT DOES GOD SAY OF ALL THESE COMMANDMENTS?

He says: "I, the Lord your God, am a jealous God, visiting the iniquity of the fathers upon the children to the third and fourth generation of those who hate me, but showing steadfast love to thousands of those who love me and keep my commandments."

What does this mean for us?

God warns that he will punish all who break these commandments. Therefore we are to fear his wrath and not disobey him. But he promises grace and every blessing to all who keep these commandments. Therefore we are to love and trust him, and gladly do what he commands.

Jealousy seems like a word better fit for soap operas and mushy love stories than the almighty God. God jealous? Can you imagine God worried sick that someone might not love him? Or playing "she loves me—she loves me not?" by picking a daisy-shaped star apart piece by piece? The God of the promise jealous?

But God uses these very words: "I, the Lord your God, am a jealous God." It's not a mistaken translation, either. In fact, if you could read Hebrew you'd find a word even stronger than jealous. The original word suggests burning like an unquenchable fire. Can you imagine that? God hot for you? Burning like a white hot flame with desire for you?

There's a more polite word for it, even if it seems tame by comparison. It is love. Lovers are the ones who get jealous. That's what stands behind God's jealousy, too. God loves you. God has made a decision about you and the whole creation: God is going to be your God and bring in the new day.

The trouble is that God has all sorts of rivals competing for you—rivals who want to come between you. Not one of them is anywhere near as great or strong as God is, of course, but that's why God is jealous. God won't tolerate anyone or anything else claiming your fear, love, and trust.

That's why God has attached a terrible threat and an even greater promise to the Ten Commandments. God makes both the threat and the promise for the same reason—out of love, in the determination to make you his own.

The threat and the promise

The threat comes first: "I, the Lord your God, am a jealous God, visiting the iniquity of the fathers upon the children to the third and fourth generation of those who hate me." That's strong medicine. In fact, it sounds unfair—that children should suffer not only for the sins of their parents but of their grandparents, great-grandparents, and great-great-grandparents.

You know by now, though, that the old self is no joke. If the sinner in us isn't anywhere near as strong as God, it is still powerful enough to hold us in a grip we can't break.

The old Adam or Eve in us makes us concerned first, foremost, and always about ourselves. It is the one who frightens and worries us, convincing us that if we don't look out for ourselves, no one else will. In each of the Commandments now, you've seen how it struggles, squirms, and fights in us to put itself between God and us and between our neighbors and ourselves. If it ever got completely out of hand, doing everything it wished in us and others, it would split the earth into billions of pieces.

To prevent that, and to keep the earth ready for the promise, God has given us the Commandments. God ties such an awful threat to them for the same reason. Because the old self is so selfish, the only way it will listen is if it knows something terrible is going to happen to it if it doesn't stop. So God threatens. It's as if God says, "Look, if you're going to insist on your selfish ways, you're going to live with the consequences."

God is far too kind to ever let us live with all of the consequences of the old sinner's work in us. But God won't be mocked, either. Nor will God spoil us, coming like an overly indulgent father or mother to bail us out of whatever scraps we get ourselves into. If you treat your parents or guardians with contempt and disobey them, God isn't going to prevent them from punishing you. In fact, God encourages them to hold you responsible for your actions. If you kill someone, God isn't going to come to the police station to plead for your release. You have to live with the results of what you do.

The consequences can keep going, too. For instance, when fathers, mothers, or guardians sin against their children by not giving them the proper love and care, the children are hurt by it. When they become parents themselves, it is hard for them to learn how to give the kind of love and care to their children they didn't get from their own parents. Thus the grandchildren can be hurt by what their grandparents did to their parents.

God isn't keeping books, looking to get even with you for something your great-great-grandpa or grandma did. God graciously forgives, never letting us live with all the consequences of wrong. But God lets us live with enough of them to let us know that these aren't empty threats. As long as the old self in you insists on selfishness, you'll have to live with its results. It is as if God says, "If you won't listen to these Commandments for my sake, listen to them for your own. If you don't, you're on your own."

God uses the promise attached to the Commandments in the same way. But the promise is much bigger than the threat:

"I, the Lord your God, am a jealous God . . . showing steadfast love to thousands of those who love me and keep my commandments." That's quite a difference, isn't it? Iniquity to three or four generations—steadfast love to thousands?

But it almost sounds as if God is trying to make a deal, promising to "show steadfast love" in exchange for love and keeping the Commandments. Is that it? What's going on here?

God knows what's up, that the old sinner in us can never resist a bargain. So God takes hold of the selfishness in us and says, "Look, if you won't hear the Commandments for my sake, listen to them for your own good. I'm going to show mercy to thousands of generations of those who love me. If you want to get in on it, you'd better give it a try."

Both the threat and the promise have the same purpose, then. God puts them together with the Commandments as parents put punishments and rewards together with their commands. They are temporary measures to hold the old self in line while the new you comes forth.

While their children are young and don't know any better, good parents give commands, telling the children what they should and shouldn't do. The parents back up their commands with punishments and rewards when they need to, making sure that their children don't hurt themselves and others.

All the while, though, the parents are looking forward to the day when commands, punishments, and rewards won't be necessary anymore. Then the children will be mature enough to know what is good and right themselves.

That's what God is looking forward to for us. For the time being, while the old self is at work, God gives the Commandments, using threats and promises to back them up. God uses them to protect us from ourselves and our neighbors, keeping the creation ready for the promise.

One day God is going to put the old sinner in us to death permanently and make the whole world new. Then Christ will reign and there will be no more old self, no more death, no more commands, threats, or bargains. Then, as Luther says in his explanation to the Sacrament of Holy Baptism, he will raise us up as his new people to "live with God in righteousness and purity forever."

Jean-Claude Lejeune

The promise and the purpose

In the meantime, the Ten Commandments are precious gifts for us. Through them, we see how God cares for us day by day, showing both promise and purpose for us.

The most important commandment by far is the First. It is "the clasp that holds the wreath together," as Luther called it. In it, God gives us his word to be our God, give us everything good, and care for us at all times. "I am the Lord your God," God says. "You shall have no other gods."

All the rest of the Commandments follow from this one. Because God promises to be our God, God gives us his name and speaks to us through the Word. Because God is our God, God protects our lives in every way, seeing to it that not only life itself but everything we need to live—including faithful companions, property, good names, and sound hopes—is kept for us.

At the same time, the First Commandment opens up all the others to show us God's purposes for us. Because God promises to be our God, God expects us to fear, love, and trust him above all things. And because God is our God, God also expects us to care for our neighbors, protecting and helping them.

Jesus summed up these purposes and all the Commandments in two: " 'You shall love the Lord your God with all your heart, and with all your soul, and with all your mind,' " he said. And " 'You shall love your neighbor as yourself.' On these two commandments hang all the law and the prophets" (Matthew 22:37, 39-40). That's why we're made; these are our purposes for living.

When the old self hears such big commandments and sees such huge purposes, it ignores the promise and starts complaining about the load. "How can God expect so much?" it asks with a scowl. "I could never do all that."

"That's right," God says, "you can't." There isn't a man, woman, or child alive who can keep these Commandments as they are meant to be kept, perfectly and completely.

God is at work

But God isn't waiting for us to keep them under our own steam, as if the Commandments were blanks on a test we had to fill in before God would care for us. God has already decided what to do with us, and has been at work since our Baptisms to do it. God is putting the old Adam or Eve in each of us to death and raising us up as new people.

That's what we're going to be—new people. God is making the new you in you, the you who will be a believer, the you who fears, loves, and trusts him. God is making the new you in you who will be a lover, one who loves the neighbor. God is making the new you in you who will be what Adam and Eve were made to be, people who care for the earth.

But now there are some questions left. How do we know that God's decision is for us? And how is God going to make us what we will be? We'll discuss these questions as we consider the Apostles' Creed. It, too, is packed full and running over with God's promises. It is a joyous declaration of how God cares for us as our creator, of all that he does for us in Christ, and of how God sends his Spirit to make and keep the new you.

Jim Whitmer

THE CREED

11
I BELIEVE

The God who has decided to be your God is different. This God, the one who said, "I am the Lord your God," is like a woman who lost a coin, turned the whole house over looking for it, and then had a big party to celebrate finding it. Or this God is like a shepherd, a pretty unusual one, who left 99 sheep unguarded in the wilderness to go looking for a lost lamb that strayed off someplace (Luke 15:3-10). It is this God, your God, who is coming looking for you.

Because God is so warmhearted, God is a little uncomfortable with commandments. They are alright, in their own way. They provide some wonderful protection, covering with God's strong hand the most important things we need each day. They could even be called a gift of God.

But to tell the truth, God gets a little tired of saying, "You shall" or "You shall not." God does it just because the old you in each of us always thinks it can get away with something. But what God really wants to do is something else: to get beyond the dos and don'ts, to come right in beside you and care for you, for every dimension of your life. Then you can live with your shoulders straight and your head back, alert and full of joy. You can have some fun.

But what kind of God is this who keeps turning over all of our expectations? What is this unusual God really like? And how do we know all this about God? The Apostles' Creed contains the church's answer to these questions. It tells us how God has sought us out to get acquainted, of what God has done for us as our creator, as the one who has redeemed us in Christ, as the Spirit who broods over us, giving life and faith. Through the Creed, as Luther once said, we learn "to know God perfectly."

God comes out of hiding

But how does this happen? How do we get to know God? Some suppose that we get to know God as we get to know any other person. We "find" God and then use our abilities to observe and reason, to figure out what we've seen.

If we start out this way, trying on our own to get a picture of who God is, we run into a solid wall right away. "No one has ever seen God" as John says in his gospel (1:18). Not even Moses, who spoke with God on Mount Sinai, could see God's face (Exodus 33:17-23).

If we can't see God, how can we get to know God? We can't sit down with him and ask questions as we could if God were another person. We can't go places or do things together either, as you might do with someone you wanted to get acquainted with at school.

There might be a door in the wall, though. If we can't see God, maybe we can find God by looking at the world around us, observing what happens, and reasoning back from there.

Think of the order and balance in nature, for instance. Spring, summer, autumn, and winter come year after year like clock-work; birds, flowers, animals, plants, and people live in an intricate web of life; in a whole universe full of stars, moons, suns, and planets, everything works together. Surely there must be a God behind it all.

But what kind of God? That's really the question. If we ask nature for an answer, we may get one, but it may be far different from what we expect.

Nature can be beautiful—that's for sure. But there are some other things for sure, too. "Mother Nature" can be cruel and ruthless, with tornadoes, cyclones, blizzards, and earthquakes that kill and do damage. And that intricate web of life is also a web of death—animals killing and being killed in the fight to survive.

What kind of God do we find if we try to peek at God through nature? A God who can be as warm as the summer sunshine

and as beautiful as the first flower in the spring, but also as cold as winter ice and as relentless as the death of the leaves in the autumn. No wonder people who try to find God in this way use such cold and lifeless names: Supreme Being, Unmoved Mover, First Cause.

We can't see God. Though we might catch a few glimpses of God in nature or in what happens to us, we can't get a picture of who God is or what God really does in this way. Trying to know God on our own terms, by our observations and reasoning, we run smack into a wall we can't break through.

It is God's own wall we run into—a wall of mirrors. You remember how the old self operates. It is the old you in you who always wants to go it alone, to have you figure out things for yourself, without help from God or your neighbors. It wants to find God for its own purposes, either to put God away or to give God some use.

That's why God has put up this wall of mirrors. When the old Adam or Eve tries to get God's measure, to pry into God's secrets, to get a jump somehow, God shines the mirrors in its face so that the only picture the old sinner in us gets is of itself.

What about it, then? Are we stymied before we start? How are we going to get to know God at all, much less perfectly, if God is hidden behind a wall of mirrors?

We cannot get to know God on our own, by our own reason or strength, effort or understanding. But if God *makes himself known*, helping us to know what God we have, then we can know God better than we know our own selves.

God does just that. God doesn't play hide and seek. Neither does God play hard to get, like a bashful stranger, hoping we'll try to get acquainted and then backing off. Rather, God makes himself known, telling us who and what we can expect from him.

If you remember the Second and Third Commandments, you already have a pretty good idea of how God does this. God makes himself known through the Word and in the things the Word does as God goes to work with people like Abraham and Sarah, Ruth and the prophets. But above all, God makes himself known in Christ.

In Christ, God became one of us, like us, our own flesh and blood. In Christ, God took upon himself the most wretched and terrifying things we know, suffering, dying, going all the way to the grave for us. In Christ, God shattered death's chains and broke the grave wide open, raising him from the dead. In Christ, God released the Spirit to bring home the Word for us, making us faithful people.

A word that works

That's how God makes himself known to us. He did what God does, God "did" himself, for us, being the kind of God who gives without holding anything back, doing what God does.

What kind of God is God then? In Christ, we learn that God knows even the sparrows and every hair of your head. God is the one who gives eyes to the blind, ears to the deaf, voices to the mute, legs to the lame, health to the sick, life to the dead. The God who raised Jesus from the dead is the one who loves his enemies, the unrighteous and the impious and the super righteous and the super pious alike. In Christ, we meet the God who forgives and raises the dead, the one who by word and deed makes all things new. God is God.

Once we begin to know what God is like in Christ, we can begin to see God's hand more clearly in the things around us. Apart from Christ, the world around us can look like a collection of accidents and coincidences that runs by luck.

Christ doesn't wipe away the mystery, telling us why things happen the way they do, why there is suffering, death, anguish, and pain. But he does tell us who it is that made our world and daily cares for it—his Father, and ours. That makes all the difference.

God doesn't just tell us about creation, giving us another science lesson. God *does* creation, making the earth and caring for it. God clothes the lilies of the field, feeds the birds of the

Jean-Claude Lejeune

air, and gives you what you need, guarding and protecting you from day to day. God is himself when God does what God alone is good at, when creating something out of nothing, when making all things new.

When we see how God makes himself known to us in Christ, we learn something else about God's heart: that God wants to be closer to us than the next thought that enters our heads. In fact, speaking a word of life and love, of hope and courage, God wants to take a hand in shaping those thoughts.

So he sends his Spirit, the Holy Spirit, to make himself known through his Word. God "does" himself again, telling the story of Jesus to us, so that our heads and hearts, hands and feet will be taken up into God's work.

What is God like? God is the God who promises and keeps his word. God is like no other person, no thing, no power you have ever known. For this God can do anything but sit still, at least where you are concerned. Like the woman with the lost coin or the shepherd with a lost lamb, God comes looking for you.

So God repeats himself, doing himself three times to tell you who he is, what he does, and what you can expect from God. For this is God, the Father almighty, creator of heaven and earth; Jesus Christ, his only Son, our Lord; the Holy Spirit. This is the triune God, one in three, three in one.

God makes himself known so that each of us can say, "I believe." That's what the Apostles' Creed is for, too. It is a very ancient creed. Most of it was put together by A.D. 340 and probably even earlier. It has been used ever since, with only a few additions in the early centuries of the church, for the same purpose: to tell people who are about to be baptized or who have been baptized who God is and what we receive and can expect from God.

The Creed was said at your Baptism, too. It was said in confidence that God was making and will make you one of his own, enabling you yourself to say, "I believe."

That isn't always easy to say. In fact, it can be very difficult. The old Adam or Eve hangs around our necks, trying to squeeze the faith out of us. It fills us with fear, despair, and pride in ourselves. It fills our world with suffering, pain, and death.

Seeing that, watching what goes on in the world, it can be hard to believe the promise, even impossible.

But that's what God is looking for, and that's what God is going to make of you: a believer. In the Commandments, we saw how God keeps the old sinner in us on a leash to protect us and keep the world ready for the promise. Now, in the Creed, we're going to see how the old you dies.

We're going to discover something else, too: how God makes himself known to raise up the new you in us, the new you who is a believer and can say, "I believe in God, the Father almighty," in "Jesus Christ, his only Son, our Lord," and in "the Holy Spirit."

Whoever can say that is being brought back to the point where Adam and Eve fell. In fact, as God enables you to say that, you are brought even further: to the point where you know God perfectly, who God is, what God does, and what you can confidently expect from God. Think it will happen? Just wait.

12
NOT HOW BUT WHO

THE FIRST ARTICLE

I believe in God, the Father almighty, creator of heaven and earth.

What does this mean?

I believe that God has created me and all that exists. He has given me and still preserves my body and soul with all their powers. He provides me with food and clothing, home and family, daily work, and all I need from day to day. God also protects me in time of danger and guards me from every evil. All this he does out of fatherly and divine goodness and mercy, though I do not deserve it. Therefore I surely ought to thank and praise, serve and obey him. This is most certainly true.

Would you like to see a miracle? Look in the mirror! Do you think that sounds strange? Look a little more closely. If you do, you'll see gifts—gifts enough to make you want to want to sing, but gifts enough to make the old you nervous, more than nervous, resentful. God can handle it all—thanks, nerves, resentment, even outright rebellion. For God is God, the one who created you and all that exists.

So take a look. There you are, growing, changing, developing, stretching away from childhood and already on the edge of becoming an adult. What do you see? You've gotten taller maybe, heavier perhaps, stronger, or more delicate. There have been some changes in you. And you've discovered some talents about you. You can sing, tell a story, run or throw, help a friend, cook a meal, plane a board, take a picture, get a laugh.

And when you move out beyond yourself, other gifts appear: family, perhaps, or a friend, a beautiful autumn day or a snappy winter's morning, the smell of buds, the taste of honey, the sound of music, a good game. Once you begin to catch a sense of the giftedness in things, gifts pop out everywhere.

So you say, with the church across the world echoing your words, "I believe in God, the Father almighty, creator of heaven and earth." But you may say something else, too: How? How does this all work?

There are good reasons for asking. Knowing how God makes life could open the door to more of nature's secrets. Knowledge might give more confidence, too. For things aren't always as easy as the words of the explanation seem. Some people have far more than they need. And there are some people who, whether they work or not, don't ever seem to get ahead.

Jean-Claude Lejeune

There's another question that you might want to ask: Who? Who really does all of this? The explanation says, without stopping to catch its breath: God. But is this true? After all, food and clothing, home and family don't just show up at the door, in a celestial delivery truck. There are parents or guardians who must provide. And the circumstances have to be right. There has to be rainfall or the economy has to be working or the new job has to come or the bills have to be paid. And there are others involved, too: teachers, police officers, coaches, counselors, directors and assistants, governmental representatives, judges, pharmacists, farmers—the list goes on.

Who is in charge? How does it work? Who makes all of this happen?

The God who has decided to be your God, the one who raised Jesus from the dead and is now at work to make all things new, is a lot more interested in promises than theories. So the Scriptures and the Creed don't do a lot of explaining. They simply make the promise again, telling you the basics of who and how, but leaving plenty for you to investigate in other ways.

God created the heavens and the earth: that's who. As the book of Genesis tells it, God spoke and it was so, bringing worlds and peoples, plants and animals to life by word of mouth. God said, "Let there be light!" and the lights came on. God breathed into the dust and there was a person and then more people—men and women. And God unfolded before them a full world.

God has been creating ever since, though now the miracle is hidden. So the how isn't quite so spectacular. Now life doesn't begin with the sound of God's voice, but with the coming together of parents. Now food begins in the quiet miracles of fertile fields and a good climate. Clothing is cut and sewn and arrives in a store through the work of people who are willing to give their skills for a paycheck. And homes, small or large, in the country or in a high rise, are built by carpenters.

God makes us hands or channels for God's purposes. In our work, God is at work making sure that what we do does some good for the people around us. So God feeds the world through the work of farmers, protects from disease through nurses and doctors, gives protection through the courts—every job, every service that is helpful has God behind it.

So God gets the job done. The one who promises to take charge of your future is the one who created you and all that exists, who has given and still preserves—who fusses over you, making sure that you are guarded and protected just because, being God, God wants to make sure you have what you need.

The old you's answer

All this talk of gifts is enough to make the old sinner in you more than a little nervous, in fact, downright nasty. "Now wait a minute," it says, stamping a foot or narrowing an eye. "Just a second here. What makes you so sure. That's not the way things work when I'm around. I'll tell you how it does: God helps those who help themselves, and I intend to do a little helping. In fact, I can handle this myself."

That's what Adam and Eve said, too: "We would rather handle this ourselves."

When God created Adam and Eve, God gave them gifts and limits. God gave them the promise to be their God; God gave them one another, the earth, and its animals for companionship; God gave them the responsibility to take care of the creation. But God gave them some limits, among them one condition: They could not eat of the tree of the knowledge of good and evil (Genesis 2:17).

When the serpent came to talk things over, it had a different idea. It wanted Adam and Eve to take the gifts without the limits, to take charge of their own futures. So the serpent asked, "Did God give you any limits?" and then set its wily trap: "You will not die," it said. "For God knows that when you eat of it [the fruit of the tree] your eyes will be opened, and you will be like God, knowing good and evil" (Genesis 3:4-5). "Just eat," the snake said, "and you'll be able to get everything you need for yourselves, without help and without restriction. You'll know what's good for you and what's bad for you and you'll be in charge. You'll be able to look after yourself."

Sometimes this has been called the story of the fall. But it is more a rise than a fall, a rise into rebellion. Adam and Eve rose up against God, trying to get control of the force of life so that they could shape and control it themselves. So they became God's enemies.

That's how the old you in each of us operates. From the day we're born until the last moment we draw breath, the old Adam or Eve in us insists that we know best—that our will, what we want, and what we like is all that matters.

"What's wrong with this?" the old sinner in us replies. "If we don't take care of ourselves, who will? Why should God get mad about that? Shouldn't we look after ourselves?"

God has an answer: "You keep your hands off of your future," God says, "because that's my business." Only the God of the promise can talk to you like this, because this God—the God of Abraham and Sarah, of Joseph and Mary and the empty grave—has decided to be your God and make a life for you. God knows that all of our attempts to go it alone come at the expense of somebody else—God's expense, the neighbor's expense, the expense of the earth. That's trouble.

But more: God loves to create. It is one of the things God is good at. So there are kangaroos and rhinos, hissing ostriches and lowing cattle; there is rhubarb and there are oranges, mangoes and popcorn; there are chocolates, dark and luscious, just waiting to be made into candy or frosting.

And there are people, tall and short, fast and slow, light and dark, fat and skinny, beautiful and not quite as nice.

CLEO Freelance Photo

There are toenails; there is ear wax; there is hair that hangs to a woman's waist and a man's head that has become as smooth as chrome.

There are fields and forests, mountains and valleys; great, wide plains spreading in all their magnificence toward the sun and valleys so narrow they are called coulees; city streets so hot in the afternoon sun they can slow down a bicycle tire and sidewalks with weeds sticking their life up through the cracks.

And there is you: the miracle of you. Once you were nothing but the gleam in two people's eyes. And then you began to take shape, growing, developing, changing, until you filled your mother's belly to overflowing. And then there you were, looking like your mom or dad, treasured by the ones who took you home, cared for night and day. And here you are: too big for any of them to handle.

"I believe that God has created me and all that exists. . . ." When God is going about the business of being God, when God is doing what God is really good at, God creates. And then there's a you, a new you, one that can't help but chuckle with wonder at all the great things God makes.

13
MYSTERY MAN

THE SECOND ARTICLE

I believe in Jesus Christ, his only Son, our Lord. He was conceived by the power of the Holy Spirit and born of the virgin Mary. He suffered under Pontius Pilate, was crucified, died, and was buried. He descended into hell. On the third day he rose again. He ascended into heaven, and is seated at the right hand of the Father. He will come again to judge the living and the dead.

What does this mean?

I believe that Jesus Christ-true God, son of the Father from eternity, and true man, born of the virgin Mary-is my Lord. At great cost he has saved and redeemed me, a lost and condemned person. He has freed me from sin, death, and the power of the devil-not with silver or gold, but with his holy and precious blood and his innocent suffering and death. All this he has done that I may be his own, live under him in his kingdom, and serve him in everlasting righteousness, innocence, and blessedness, just as he is risen from the dead and lives and rules eternally. This is most certainly true.

The best way to ruin a good mystery story is to read the end before finishing the rest of it. Whether it is a book, comic book, or rerun on television, knowing how the story is going to turn out usually takes the fun out of it.

Some mysteries are different, though, especially good ones. They can tell you what the end of the story will be and still keep you on the edge of your chair wondering who really did it and how it happened.

The story of Jesus is like that. You already know the end of it, that Jesus was crucified, died, and was buried; that he was raised from the dead and will bring in the new creation. But knowing the end of the story doesn't take the mystery away. In fact, it may just make him and his story all the more mysterious.

Who is Jesus? What kind of person is he? And what really happened in him?

How do you get to know other people? By seeing them and hearing them, right? Or, if you can't do that, by listening to others who have seen or heard them.

That's one way we can learn something about Jesus. Though we can't see him or talk with him as we could if he were someone in the congregation or at school, we can listen to what the gospels tell us people saw and heard in him. If we do, we'll get taken up in the mystery.

One of the first things the gospels tell us about Jesus is that he was a person, a human being. That's how the gospels speak of him, and that's how the people he walked and talked with saw him. They saw a real man. "Where did this man get this wisdom and these deeds of power?" the people of Nazareth asked. "Is not this the carpenter's son? Is not his mother called Mary? And are not his brothers James and Joseph and Simon and Judas? And are not all his sisters with us? Where then did this man get all this?" (Matthew 13:54-56).

He was a man. That's part of what made him such a mystery.

The Creed insists on it, too: that no matter what else can and should be said about Jesus, he was a real live human being. He was "born of the virgin Mary," the Creed says. The most important word is *born*—born as you were born, as all human beings are born. So, as the explanation in the Catechism says, he was "true man," a real person.

But what kind of person? One of the next things the gospels tell us about him is that he was a preacher. That's what Jesus did.

As Mark tells about Jesus' preaching, he had a message that said, "The time is fulfilled," Jesus said, "and the kingdom of God has come near; repent, and believe

Kenneth C. Poertner

in the good news" (Mark 1:15). He proclaimed and promised it again and again: that God himself is coming to make the new you and the new creation.

"The Spirit of the Lord is upon me," Jesus said, reading from the book of Isaiah to the people in Nazareth, "because he has anointed me to bring good news to the poor. He has sent me to proclaim release to the captives and recovery of sight to the blind, to let the oppressed go free, to proclaim the year of the Lord's favor" (Luke 4:18-19).

That's just exactly what Jesus did. He brought good news to the poor, going from town to town and table to table, telling all kinds of people about God's decision. He proclaimed release to the old Adam and Eve's captives—religious people who fancied themselves in some kind of special favor with God, irreligious people who were despised and condemned. He gave prostitutes a new start. He sat and ate with tax collectors like Zacchaeus who had made a fortune cheating, and radicals like Simon the Zealot, one of his disciples, who wanted to start a revolution to drive out all the Romans.

Wherever Jesus went, he made people new. He gave sight to those who were blind—people like Bartimaeus who sat begging by the roadside as Jesus went to Jerusalem. He let people who were oppressed go free—like the paralyzed man who was lowered to him through the roof of a house or like the men whose bodies were rotten with the disease of leprosy and couldn't enjoy the company of others because of their illness. He healed the sick and raised the dead, driving out demons and making people new by just saying the word.

That's what made Jesus such a mystery, not only to the people of Nazareth but to others wherever he went. That's what can make him so mysterious to us, too. He was a man—nobody who saw him had any doubt about that. He was a preacher—everybody who heard him knew that, too.

But how could he make people new by just saying the word? Who was he, that he could stride through Galilee preaching God's decision about his people and his creation?

Not even his family and disciples—the people who thought they knew him best—could figure him out completely. His family once tried to seize him and take him home (Mark 3:21). And his disciples misunderstood him again and again (Mark 8:14-21, for instance).

Other preachers and teachers in Israel, as well as the Romans, had an answer, though. To them he was more than a mystery. He was a threat. The religious leaders took Jesus for a blasphemer, a false preacher who takes God's name in vain.

The Romans apparently took him for another radical freedom fighter. They were the only ones in Israel who could condemn a man to death. And that's what they did. He suffered under the authority of Pontius Pilate, the Roman governor. He was crucified, died, and was buried—put to death the way runaway slaves, criminals, and rebels were killed.

Who does he think he is?

There's another way we could try to get to the bottom of the mystery. We could try to figure out from the gospels who Jesus thinks he is. That works with some people. You can come straight out and ask, "Who are you?" and get an answer. If we do that with Jesus, though, the mystery only deepens.

The mystery is that in only one verse in the first three gospels does Jesus come right out and say that he is the Christ, the Messiah. Other people often say that he is. For instance, when Jesus asked his disciples, "Who do you say that I am?" Peter replied, "You are the Messiah" (Mark 8:29). And after he was crucified, the captain of the Roman soldiers who put him to death said, "Truly this man was God's Son" (Mark 15:39).

But Jesus said it only once, and then in a puzzling way. When Jesus was on trial, the high priest asked him, "Are you the Messiah, the Son of the Blessed One?" And Jesus said, "I am; and 'you will see the Son of Man seated at the right hand of the Power,' and 'coming with the clouds of heaven'" (Mark 14:61-62).

It's almost as if Jesus shrugged his shoulders and said, "Sure I am, but just wait until you see the Son of man coming. That will really be something." It sounds as though Jesus was trying to make it mysterious.

Sometimes people don't talk about themselves for good reason—it sounds like bragging. Jesus said as much himself: "If I testify about myself, my testimony is not true" (John 5:31). Maybe instead of talking about himself, he let us know who he is in another way: by what he did.

Just run through the gospels, watching what Jesus does. He goes all over Galilee and finally to Jerusalem preaching God's decision and promise to make the new creation. He heals the sick, drives out demons, forgives sins, and raises the dead, making people new wherever he finds them. And when he gets to Jerusalem, he doesn't fight or organize the disciples to protect him. He surrenders and lets the people who want to do away with him carry him to his death.

The clue

That's the clue: to watch what Jesus does and what happens to him. When you do, you'll see an entirely different kind of person—the new Adam. Where the old Adam is always trying to take care of himself, to get and grab as much as possible, Jesus lets go of himself, putting himself out for us. He reverses the old Adam or Eve's direction, giving himself completely instead of trying to hold on to himself.

We'll follow up this clue in the next chapter. In the meantime, while we've run into a mystery, we've gained some important information.

Jesus was a man, a real live human being—in fact, as the new Adam, the only truly human being. Jesus was a preacher—one who proclaimed God's promise and put the promise into action, making all kinds of people new. He didn't say very much about who he is, but let his action do the talking for him.

14
FRIEND OF SINNERS

Who is Jesus? So far, we have a mystery and a clue. He was a man, and he was a preacher.

But he was amazing. Jesus not only said that God had decided to make his creation new; he went to work all over Galilee and finally in Jerusalem doing just that, making people new. Who in the world was he that he could say and do such amazing things? That's the question, the mystery of Jesus.

We have one big clue to go on. As much as he said, Jesus would also let his action do some talking. The clue, then, is to keep eyes open and ears to the ground to catch the action in his story—what Jesus does and what happens to him.

When we do that, we run into the biggest events in Jesus' story: the cross and the resurrection. There's a lot of mystery here, too, but Good Friday and Easter throw light on the whole story of Jesus. They tell us who he is and what happened in him, how the old Adam or Eve dies as the new you is born and the new age begins.

The lights of Easter

Jesus was dead. He hung on the cross until he died. When the soldiers took him down to haul his body away, they made sure there was no mistake about it, spearing him in the side to drain the lifeblood out of him. His body was taken and buried in another man's tomb, sealed in a cave behind a stone.

The disciples and those who had followed Jesus thought it was the end of the mystery. They thought he was just one more good man who had said and done some amazing things but who had died like everyone else.

Jesus knew the fear death brings. At Gethsemane the night before, Mark says, Jesus was "distressed and agitated" (14:33), praying three times that it wouldn't be necessary to suffer and die in such a way. And when he did die, Jesus cried out in pain and agony, "My God, my God, why have you forsaken me?" (15:34). He wasn't pretending or just giving up his life for a weekend. He died.

Like the disciples, Mary Magdalene, Mary the mother of James, and Salome also thought the mystery was over when they went to the grave on Easter morning. They didn't go to see if Jesus really would be raised. They went to wash his body with oils and spices so that it wouldn't smell of death.

When they got there, the women got the surprise of their lives—the biggest surprise in all of history. The tomb was empty. Jesus had been raised from the dead. He is risen. Later on, others saw and spoke with him. He appeared to Peter and the disciples, to 500 of those who had followed him, to James and the apostles, and finally to Paul (1 Corinthians 15:3-8).

Now there is a lot of mystery in the resurrection, too. All kinds of fascinating questions can be asked about it. But in all of the mystery, two things are most important: that Jesus was crucified and that God raised him from the dead.

Together, these events are like the sun. Though we can't look at them directly, with naked eyes, we can see the light they shed. Good Friday and Easter light up the mystery, telling us who Jesus is and why he died. And they light up the future, the dawning of the new age.

When the disciples saw and heard Jesus risen from the dead, they set out to preach him to all who would listen. They proclaimed him in a short and simple creed: "Jesus is Lord."

That's the light the resurrection sheds on the mystery of who Jesus is. He is Lord, God himself in the flesh of a person like us, God being himself, doing what God does, for us. Jesus is "true God, Son of the Father from eternity," as the explanation in the Catechism says.

Why all the mystery, then? Why didn't Jesus come right out at the beginning and say himself that he is God?

"If I testify about myself, my testimony is not true," Jesus said (John 5:31). But there's more to it, too. Do you love someone who is always lording it over you, telling you what you have to do whether you like it or not? Someone who is always pushing you around, trying to prove physical superiority?

Can you see it now? God is making believers, people who will love him wholeheartedly, for himself, with nothing held back.

How's God going to make that kind of love? Not with force. Love can't be forced. Not by scaring you. You don't love people who scare you. No, God will get it by setting aside all of his power, glory, honor, and might to become a person, just like you, as he has done in Christ. By becoming a person who laughs and who struggles, as you do; by becoming poor, weak, humble, and sorrowful, as we often are; by sitting down to the table and taking food with the wretched and despised—prostitutes, traitors, radicals, cowards, pretenders, the unrighteous, and the ungodly of all kinds. That's just what Jesus did.

J. Michael Fitzgerald

The cross was no mistake

But why did he have to die, then? In the light of Easter, we can see that, too. In Christ, God wasn't willing to go halfway for us. He went all the way, giving himself completely, withholding nothing, to break the old self's grip and make us his own. The cross wasn't a mistake or an accident. It happened on purpose, the way Christ wanted it to.

What would happen to you if the police found you with some others who had stolen some things? Even if you were completely innocent, you would be accused of the same crime. You would become what the law sometimes calls an "accessory after the fact," a befriender of criminals. And you would be liable for the thieves' punishment. That's the way the law works.

If you were picked up like that, more than likely you'd yell and protest, telling everybody who would listen how unfair it is to be accused of something you didn't do. But what if you really loved the people you were with? That would make quite a difference, wouldn't it?

That was Jesus' "crime": his love. He kept bad company. He wanted to be the friend of sinners—not only of thieves, prostitutes, tax collectors, revolutionaries, and other criminals, but of all kinds of sinners. And when he was condemned to die for it, Jesus didn't go kicking and screaming to the cross, crying out about the unfairness of it. Though it was a dreadful suffering and a horrible death, he *wanted* it that way, to take upon himself the sins, punishment, and death of his friends, his people— each of us. He bore our sins in his body.

Jesus gave himself like a loving mother would give herself if she threw herself in front of a speeding car to protect her child playing in the street. Jesus gave himself like a soldier covering an explosion to protect his friends. Jesus put his body on the line, sacrificing himself for us.

That's the key. Jesus' death isn't a sacrifice to God; it is God's sacrifice for us. Jesus laid down his life for us, giving everything, withholding nothing, dying condemned and abandoned, to set us free. That is love—love that "does not insist on its own way," that "does not rejoice in wrongdoing, but rejoices in the truth," that "bears all things" for us (1 Corinthians 13:5-7).

Jim Whitmer

The new you and the new age

Someday you will die, as Jesus did—not on a cross, most likely, but somewhere, somehow. Sometimes it can seem far away, sometimes close at hand and frightening. But it's the way life works now. Every living thing, no matter what or who it is, must die.

In Christ's word, the word of his death and resurrection, you hear a new word that breaks the power of death. It is a word spoken by the same God who created the heavens and the earth, the same God who became a person, who suffered and died and was raised from the dead in Christ.

This new word is a promise: Though you die, you will live. It is the word of the cross and Easter: As Christ died for you, he lives for you to make you and his creation new. That's the light that shines into the future, lighting it up for you, showing you what is to come.

Christ's death and resurrection are the old Adam or Eve's death. It is like a great battle. Christ came armed with grace and truth and every blessing. The old sinner in us came armed with sin and death and every curse, determined to get rid of God forever. Jesus took the old sinner on in his own body and said, "Alright, do your worst. Put me to death and just see where it gets you." Then, just when the old Adam or Eve was leaning back, confident that by death Christ had been destroyed, Jesus was raised from the dead. "Death," Jesus said, "it's your turn. Now you die."

Christ's death and resurrection are the beginning of a new people, the birth of the new age. Christ is the new Adam, the "pioneer and perfecter of our faith," as Hebrews calls him (12:2). He is the only one who kept the First Commandment completely, counting on God to deliver him and give him everything good, even into the grave. He is the only one who gave himself for his neighbors completely, for us. Now God has raised him from the dead, the first one who is what Adam and Eve were made to be. Now he is at work to make you and all of his people what he is: completely new.

The old Adam or Eve dies and the new you comes forth each time that you hear this word, the word of Christ's cross and resurrection. It is the word of freedom for you—freedom "from sin, death, and the power of the devil," as the explanation of the Second Article says. When Christ speaks it to you, he sets you free to be, to be what God made you to be.

As long as the old self lives, it tries to make it seem that God is your enemy—some kind of faraway judge you can ignore completely or have to appease by doing good things. Then you play God yourself, pretending you have to take care of yourself, worrying about whether you're going to get what you want and need.

But when you hear Christ's word, that changes. For then you know that God is not your enemy, but your true Father—the one who in Christ has given himself completely for you, withholding nothing. As you hear this, the old sinner in you dies and you can say, "That's it. I don't want to be my own god anymore. I want you to be my God and to keep your promises to me."

Dale D. Gehman

When this happens, you know what the name *God* means at last, who God is, and what kind of God you have. You know that the God who has decided for you is the Lord of all things and every moment, the one who will give you everything good, come what may; that the God we know in Christ is the God who doesn't hold out or hold back. And then you can speak to him as Jesus did, calling God "Abba! Dear Father!" "Daddy." For God is your God, your heavenly father, who is even closer than your own parents.

Your neighbors change, too, as you hear Christ's word. As long as the old self is alive and kicking in you, it makes your neighbors seem like competitors or rivals to you. They are either so unimportant that you couldn't care less about them, or they become so terribly important to you that you worry and wonder always about what they think of you.

But as you hear Christ's word, your neighbors become neighbors again, real neighbors. They are Christ's friends and yours—people you can help, care for, and enjoy; people who will help, care for, and enjoy you.

Christ's word changes the earth for you, too. To the old self, the earth is a dump full of resources and raw materials to be taken, used, and exploited for self-satisfaction. But as Christ makes you new with his word, the earth becomes God's garden for you. The land, the trees, the sky, the plants, and the animals become gifts to you—gifts to love, to cherish, to protect and care for as God's own.

That's what Adam and Eve were made for; in Christ that's what the new you is going to be: one who takes God at his word, who loves the neighbor, and cares for the earth.

But now the old Adam or Eve doesn't just drop dead. As long as we live, it keeps struggling for little resurrections of its own, trying to take over again. It threatens us with our own deaths, trying to make it appear that dying is all we have to look forward to. And it tempts us in every way possible, working to replace confidence in God with doubt, love of the neighbor with animosity, and care of the earth with disregard for it. Wherever and whenever the old self succeeds, there is fear and doubt, worry and struggle and defeat.

The old you's number is up, though. As Christ defeated it with his cross and resurrection, he defeats the old self now with his word. And he is going before us into the future to establish his kingdom and bring in the new day. Then the old sinner in us will be dead forever, and we will all be new.

In the meantime, bearing Christ's word and awaiting his new day is like playing in the last part of a game that has already been won. The old self can do some damage and score some points. But it is bound to lose. For Christ has defeated it and will defeat it. And Christ has sent his Spirit to us to uphold, comfort, and strengthen us, making us what we will be.

15
GOD THE VERB

THE THIRD ARTICLE

I believe in the Holy Spirit, the holy catholic Church, the communion of saints, the forgiveness of sins, the resurrection of the body, and the life everlasting. Amen.

What does this mean?

I believe that I cannot by my own understanding or effort believe in Jesus Christ my Lord, or come to him. But the Holy Spirit has called me through the Gospel, enlightened me with his gifts, and sanctified and kept me in true faith. In the same way he calls, gathers, enlightens, and sanctifies the whole Christian church on earth, and keeps it united with Jesus Christ in the one true faith. In this Christian church day after day he fully forgives my sins and the sins of all believers. On the last day he will raise me and all the dead and give me and all believers in Christ eternal life. This is most certainly true.

When the old self gets religion, one of its favorite tricks is trying to turn the Creed into a do-it-yourself kit. Right here, at the beginning of the Third Article, is where it strikes.

"Oh yes," the old sinner in us will say, "God supplies all the parts. God created you and sent Jesus. But now you have to finish the job. You have to accept God, you must believe in God, and do something to show you're really sincere."

Like all of the old self's tricks, this sounds reasonable. But like all of its tricks, too, this one has the same purpose: to tie us up in ourselves.

When it springs this trick, the old sinner in us uses this to convince us that we can do everything God wants by our own efforts. Then we become proud and look down on our neighbors who, we conclude, aren't doing as well as we are.

Or, if that fails, the old self springs it another way to convince us that God won't have anything to do with us because we don't seem to be able to believe. Then we wind up despairing and hopeless, ready to give up. Either way, the joy of God's promise is destroyed.

That's why the explanation of the Third Article begins on what appears to be the wrong foot: "I believe that I cannot by my own understanding or effort believe in Jesus Christ my Lord, or come to him." The old you doesn't like to hear things like this, but it's said for a purpose: It is to stop the old self in its tracks, to close the door on this trick, and to point to the gifts God gives.

It is true that we cannot believe on our own, "by our own understanding or effort." But God doesn't expect us to. The God who created you and set you free in Christ doesn't have any time for do-it-yourself kits, not where the Word and promise are concerned. When this God starts a job, the job gets finished. When this God gives gifts, they are so full of grace that a person can't help but say, "You bet! That's for me!"

That's why God has sent us the Holy Spirit. It's the Spirit who brings us God's gifts and opens us up to receive them. The Spirit works with the Word in and through the church to make us what God intends us to be: new people. What the old self wants to do alone, for itself, God insists on doing for us. That's the Spirit's work: to make us what God created us to be.

The Spirit of life

One of the things that makes the Spirit sound so mysterious is its names. When it is called the Holy Spirit or the Holy Ghost, it can almost sound as if it is some kind of mist or supernatural gas that blows around the atmosphere doing strange things.

The one who can clear up this mystery is Jesus. Before he was crucified, he promised the Spirit to his disciples and to the church. He called the Spirit the "Advocate." "And I will ask the Father," Jesus said, "and he will give you another Advocate, to be with you forever. This is the Spirit of truth" (John 14:16-17). It "will teach you everything, and remind you of all that I have said to you" (John 14:26). "When the Advocate comes, whom I will send to you from the Father, the Spirit of truth who comes from the Father, he will testify on my behalf" (John 15:26).

Jesus kept his promise, sending the Spirit to his disciples on the day of Pentecost, according to Luke. You may remember the story—the "sound like the rush of a violent wind," the "tongues, as of fire, appeared among them" (Acts 2:2-3). The gift of the Spirit changed everything for the disciples. When they received it, they started speaking in other languages and set out to tell everyone who would listen the story of Jesus' death and resurrection.

Who is the Spirit, then? The Spirit is the one who makes the story of Jesus

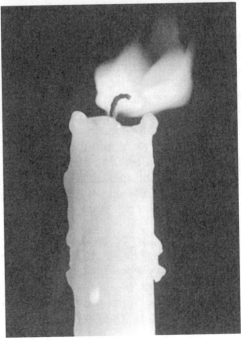

Carlin Stock Photos

103

known to us, who tells us of Christ and brings us his gifts. It is called a spirit or ghost because it is invisible, but it's not just any spirit or a ghost such as you've heard about in stories. It is God's Spirit, the Holy Spirit, the Spirit of life.

The Spirit was there when God created the heavens and the earth—"a wind from God swept over the face of the waters," as Genesis says (1:2). It was there when God "formed man from the dust of the ground, and breathed into his nostrils the breath of life" (Genesis 2:7). It was there when Jesus was baptized. Jesus "saw the heavens torn apart and the Spirit descending like a dove on him," Mark says (1:10).

The Spirit is no afterthought. The Holy Spirit is God, God being God for us again, to make God's self known to us. It is the spirit of the risen Christ, "the Lord, the giver of life," as the Nicene Creed says it. The Spirit is God at work to give us life in Christ, making us what we are going to be.

The verb

Do you remember the difference between nouns and verbs? You probably don't need another grammar lesson here, but the difference will tell you something more about the Holy Spirit. Nouns, like *chair*, sit still. They name things, telling you what they are. Verbs, like *move* or *jump*, have movement in them. They are action words. Even the quiet ones are lively.

The Spirit is a verb. Nouns don't work so well for the Spirit, for the Holy Spirit is always at work, always moving, active, making words jump and come to life. Knowing what the Spirit does, then, will tell you some more about who it is.

That's why the explanation of the Spirit's work in the Catechism is so full of verbs. The whole explanation is alive with them. What does the Spirit do? It *calls*, it *gathers*, it *enlightens*, it *sanctifies*.

First of all, the Spirit *calls*. That's what you do when you want to talk with your friends or get together with someone. You call them, whether it's on the telephone or by shouting across the street. You get word to them that you want to speak with them. The Spirit calls in the same way—with the Word, the story of Jesus. The Spirit calls you through the gospel.

105

The Spirit first called you when you were baptized, when the word of Christ's death and resurrection was first declared over you. The Spirit was sent to you at your Baptism, to call you and make you God's own. The Holy Spirit knows your name, calls you by name, and keeps right on calling you, day after day. The Spirit calls relentlessly in the preaching of the Word and the giving of the sacraments. It comes right out in the open, as at your Baptism, taking whatever risks need to be taken to give you the absolute gift. The Spirit holds nothing back. It simply says, "You are mine." That is the call.

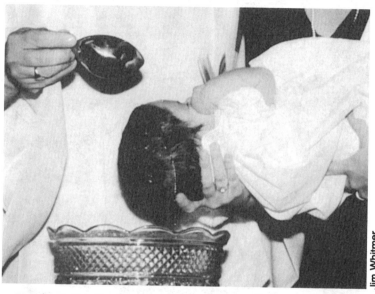

Jim Whitmer

But the Spirit likes company. So we are *gathered*, put together with other people. When you were baptized, more than likely your parents or guardians and some sponsors or some friends stood with you. As you have heard the Word preached, you have been in the company of others—your family, a whole congregation of people. As you have gone to Sunday school, it has been in groups.

That's how the Spirit gathers. The Holy Spirit doesn't make lone rangers who travel by themselves. When it says, "You belong to God," the Spirit speaks to each of us, individually.

But at the same time, the Spirit says to all of us, "You are all mine." The Holy Spirit puts us together with others, making us a part of them and them a part of us. This is the church—a people gathered together to hear the Word and receive the sacraments—a people called and gathered by the Spirit.

Having called and gathered you together with others, the Holy Spirit *enlightens* you. To enlighten something means to turn the lights on it, to light up what has been dark, to make sense out of what has been puzzling, to clear up what has been mysterious.

The Spirit has enlightened you in the same way as it has called you and gathered you together with others: with the Word. The Spirit has enlightened you through preaching, in Sunday school classes, at home during devotions. The Spirit is enlightening you now, according to Jesus' promise, using words that tell of Christ and what he does.

When the Spirit enlightens, though, you get more than a lesson. The Holy Spirit always wants to bring you to the point where you can say, "So that's who God is. So that's the way God works." But beyond that, the Spirit also will bring you to

Jim Whitmer

the point where you can say, "That's for me. I want this Word and promise." As this happens, the Spirit gets you on your way to becoming what God made you to be. The Spirit will keep enlightening you too, lighting up more and more for you as it brings forth the new you.

That brings us to one more verb: the Spirit *sanctifies.* It is a church word, one that you don't hear very often on the street or in school. It comes from an old Latin word that means "sacred" or "holy." And it sums up, in a word, everything the Spirit does, its whole purpose for us. The Spirit is making us holy, making us what God made us to be, a new people.

How is the Spirit doing this? Where does the Spirit work, and what are we going to be like when it makes us holy? These questions will have to wait until the next chapter.

In the meantime, though, we know who is working and what is being done. The old self likes to think that you can make a believer out of yourself, that you're the one who has to make yourself what God wants you to be. It can't be done. Having created us and come to us in Christ, God sends his Spirit to grace us. So the Spirit calls us, gathers us, enlightens and sanctifies us.

16
SAINTS AND SINNERS

If you were to pick out a word to describe yourself, it probably wouldn't be *holy*. You probably wouldn't call yourself a "saint," either. Whether out of fear of seeming too proud or out of knowledge of our own shortcomings, we usually don't use these words to speak of ourselves or others.

But even if *holy* and *saint* aren't words you'd choose, they describe what the Holy Spirit is making of you and what the church is. The Spirit is making you holy. And the Spirit is doing it through the Word it speaks in "the holy catholic Church," which is "the communion of saints."

Last chapter we discussed who the Spirit is and what it does. The Holy Spirit is the Spirit of life, God doing what God does for us to call, gather, enlighten, and sanctify us.

Now, in this chapter, we're going to take a look at the Spirit's workshop, its tools, and what it is making of us—holy people. The Spirit's workshop is the church. As the Spirit works in and through the church with the tools of Word and sacrament, the church is made the "communion of saints" and we are made holy.

The Spirit's workshop

It may seem like more of the old you's bragging to say that God's own Spirit is at work in the church. It doesn't take much to see that the church isn't perfect, far from it.

The church has all the faults and problems of the people who belong to it. It can be boring and routine. It can be clubby, cliquey, and downright nasty at times. The church has pretenders in it who think they're going to get to heaven by being more religious than others. And it has plenty of people who say one thing on Sunday morning and do something far different during the week.

If it depended on people, on what we say and do, to make the church what it is, it would never be holy, catholic, or a communion of saints.

But with all of our shortcomings and failings, Christ has promised that the Spirit will speak to us. "When the Advocate comes," he said, "whom I will send to you from the Father, ... he will testify on my behalf" (John 15:26). It is the Spirit's speaking, making Christ known to us, that makes the church what it is: the people of God gathered together to hear the Word and receive the sacraments.

Last chapter we discussed how the Spirit calls and gathers us. Beginning in the Sacrament of Baptism, the Holy Spirit calls us again and again through the word of Christ, saying "you are mine." And as the Spirit calls us, it never leaves us alone. The Spirit keeps putting us in the company of other people.

The Spirit calls and gathers throughout the world. Wherever it goes, the Spirit sets people apart for the gospel and brings them together with others. Though there are many small gatherings of many different kinds in many different places, there is one church. It is called the "catholic" or universal church, because it is made up of all the people the Spirit has called and gathered throughout the world: Lutherans and Roman Catholics, Presbyterians and Methodists, Christians of every shape, size, and color. The gathering of these people called by the Spirit, whether in small congregations or worldwide assemblies, is the first mark of the church.

To call and gather us, and to enlighten and sanctify us, the Spirit uses tools: the Word and the sacraments. They are the second mark of the church. For it's through them that the Spirit speaks and bestows the gifts of new life.

The Spirit speaks to us by making the Word fit for the lips of common, ordinary, everyday people—people like your pastor, your father or mother or guardians, your Sunday school teacher or catechist. As they tell you of Christ, the Spirit is at work in the Word to tell you that you are his. Wherever the

Spirit goes, God's word is spoken. And wherever God's word is spoken, the Spirit is at work in it.

With the Word, the Spirit also uses the sacraments—Baptism and the Lord's Supper. Through them, as you will see in later chapters, the Spirit gives us Christ's gifts to make us his.

That's why the church is called *holy, catholic,* and *the communion of saints.* It's not because the building is any different. Nor is it because the people in your church or you yourself are so much better than others, either.

The church is holy because the Spirit is holy and makes the church. The church is catholic because in and through it the Spirit works throughout the world to make Christ known and to give Christ's gifts. It is the communion of saints because it is the gathering of people who have been called by the Spirit and are being made saints through the Word and the sacraments.

God's saints

But now what about you? How can you be called holy or a saint? What is the Spirit making of you and the rest of us?

You are called both holy and a saint because the word the Spirit speaks to you in the church is Christ's word of forgiveness. It is pronounced each Sunday in your congregation and can be spoken to you any time you want to hear it. "Your sin is forgiven for Jesus' sake," the pastor says. Though the exact wording may vary, whenever words such as these are spoken, Christ is at work to make them work.

James L. Shaffer

111

As these words are spoken, you can be sure that the Spirit is with you to give you exactly what they say. For the Holy Spirit is the spirit of the risen Christ, the friend of sinners. When the Spirit says, "You are mine. I forgive you," all of your sin is wiped out completely. Christ doesn't just overlook it or say that it doesn't matter. He destroys it, so that there is nothing left of it. All that you have done and failed to do is forgiven.

When you hear these words, then, you can be sure that God is making you as innocent as Adam and Eve were before their rebellion. God has decided for you—God holds nothing against you. You are holy, one of his saints.

The Spirit goes even further. It not only tells you what Christ has done about your past, forgiving you all your sins, but the Spirit tells you what Christ is doing about your future, that Jesus is going to raise you from the dead.

This word is spoken to you each Sunday, too, and in the same part of the service: the absolution. For when your sins are forgiven, God pledges to make your future good—for all eternity.

Hearing this promise, you can be sure that God will do just what God says: that "on the last day he will raise [you] and all the dead and give [you] and all believers in Christ eternal life."

The Holy Spirit wants the whole you. So the Spirit is going to raise you, the real you, the whole you, the person you are. It will be "the resurrection of the body," as the Creed says, and you will be with Christ forever. For God has decided that you are one of the saints and declared you so, promising to forgive and raise you from the dead.

Now doesn't that change everything? You don't have to try to cover up where you've been wrong or failed to do right. God has forgiven you, and God will forgive you.

You don't have to be anxious, either—worrying, wondering, trying to "be like God." God has promised to raise you from the dead, to make you his very own forever.

Now, as you hear the Spirit's Word and promise, you can be what God intends you to be: one of God's new creatures. Taking God at his word, you can rely on God for everything good, fearing, loving, and trusting God above all things. Taking God at his word, you can be a neighbor, enjoying and helping the people you live and go to school and work with. Taking God at his word, you can help to care for the earth, too, enjoying and cherishing it as God's precious gift.

That's what the Spirit is making of you: a believer. The Spirit isn't interested in all our efforts to be somebody else, in pious pretense. The Spirit is making holy people, believers—laughing, loving, singing, praising, grateful people who are what God has made us to be.

It's not always so easy to believe, though, is it? Maybe you've known some times when it hasn't been difficult—some times when worries have disappeared, when you have been sure that God was caring for you, when you've enjoyed your neighbors and God's creation.

But you've also known some other kinds of times, perhaps times when questions and doubts have made it difficult to believe, times when your neighbors have seemed more like enemies than friends, times when the creation has seemed pretty hostile, or you haven't cared the slightest bit about it.

You are not yet what God made you to be. There are two yous: an old you that struggles and fights, worries, and wonders, because it is going to die, and a new you born in the water and the word of Baptism. These two yous fight within each of us, and they will keep on struggling until the old you, the old Adam or Eve, finally dies forever—when we die.

But in that struggle now, you know the promises of the Creed. You know that God, the Father almighty, the creator of heaven and earth, is your Father; that Jesus Christ, his only Son, our Lord, has taken your sin and death upon himself, becoming your friend; that the Holy Spirit is at work right now, in and through the church, speaking the word of forgiveness and the promise of the resurrection to you.

Knowing that, hearing God's promise, you can be sure that the old sinner in you is going to lose, and not only lose, but die. In all of your struggles, fears, and doubts, the Spirit is at work to make a believer out of you. And as the Spirit does this work, it will keep you, too, never letting you go. You are Christ's. And someday, when the last day comes, there will no longer be two yous but one: the new you Christ has made.

THE LORD'S PRAYER

17
CHRIST PUTS THE WORDS IN OUR MOUTHS

THE INTRODUCTION

Our Father in heaven.

What does this mean?

Here God encourages us to believe that he is truly our Father and we are his children. We therefore are to pray to him with complete confidence just as children speak to their loving father.

THE DOXOLOGY

For the kingdom, the power, and the glory are yours, now and forever. Amen.

What does "Amen" mean?

Amen means Yes, it shall be so. We say Amen because we are certain that such petitions are pleasing to our Father in heaven and are heard by him. For he himself has commanded us to pray in this way and has promised to hear us.

The good Lord would like to hear from you. Having decided to be your God—creating you, setting you free in Christ and making a saint of you—God wonders if there isn't something you need, something that might be bothering you. So God wants you to pray. It is just like the God who raised Jesus from the dead. This God doesn't ever know when to back off.

But there is something more here, too. God knows the shape your life is going to take. You are going to have times of joy and celebration. But there are going to be some tough times, too. As long as the old Adam or Eve hangs around your neck, you are going to have some struggles with yourself. The neighbors aren't always so much fun. And there are other powers you are going to have to contend with, as well.

So even as Christ has taken hold of you, you are a battle-ground—someone being fought over. You need to know how to call out to God, how to get hold of the one who has promised to help you and who will never let you down. So you have to learn how to pray.

There's no better way to learn than to study the prayer Christ himself taught us, the Lord's own prayer. We'll start out by looking at the beginning and end of it to see how it can be prayed with certainty. Than we'll look some more at how we can call God *Father*, even when the old self in us is making a mess of our prayers.

Jean-Claude Lejeune

Praying for certain

In the Commandments and the Creed, we have already seen how we can be certain that God listens to our prayers. God not only hears them, God wants us to pray, teaches us to pray, and prays for us.

First of all, we can pray because God has promised to be our God. It's the First Commandment again—"I am the Lord your God. You shall have no other gods." "I am yours," God says, "and you are mine. I have decided for you."

In Christ, God put this promise into action. God made it flesh and blood for us, becoming a person like us to become our friend and Lord. Christ went to the cross and death for us, bearing our sins in his body, to carry out the promise of the First Commandment—to make us his own people, his sons and daughters.

Because we have this promise in Christ, we can call on God for anything and everything we need. It is like getting word from the president or prime minister that says, "Give me a call if you need anything." But it is on a far bigger scale, for it is God's word and promise. Because God is your God and promises to help you, you can say to the creator of the heavens and the earth, "Dear God, you have promised—I need your help."

But second, God not only tells us that we may pray, God commands us to pray. It is as if God is talking to himself, "If I just tell them that they can pray, they might not dare to. I'll command them to pray so that they'll know how much I want them to come to me for whatever they need." Or it's like a parent, guardian, or friend saying, "Now listen. I want to help you. Call me and I'll be right there."

So in the Second Commandment, God tells us to "call on him in prayer, praise, and thanksgiving." It is a friendly command that God lovingly gives us to assure us that we not only can but should ask for God's help.

God could hardly do more than that, we might think. "I've told you that you may pray," God could have said, "and not only that, I've commanded you to pray. If you mess it up now, it's all over."

But God did more. Having given us the promise and commanded us to pray, Christ himself teaches us how to pray.

117

That's why it's called the *Lord's* Prayer. It is the prayer that Christ taught to his disciples and, through his Word, teaches to us.

Perhaps the disciples had some of the same questions and problems many of us have with prayer. Maybe praying had become an automatic routine for them. Or maybe they weren't quite sure how to act or what to say when they prayed. Whatever the reason, they asked Jesus to teach them how to pray (Luke 11:1).

There are two versions of the Lord's Prayer. One is in Matthew 6:9-13 and the other is in Luke 11:2-4. We use the version found in Matthew. The Doxology, "For the kingdom, the power, and the glory are yours, now and forever" isn't in either Matthew or Luke but has been part of the Lord's Prayer ever since the first century.

The fact that it is Jesus who teaches us this prayer is most important. Jesus is *Emmanuel*, God with us. When Jesus teaches us to pray, he knows what he's talking about—he's the one whom God sent to bring home the promise for us, making it possible for us to pray.

So Jesus was sent by the one whose name we pray will be hallowed, the one whose kingdom will come and whose will be done, the one who gives us our daily bread and forgives us our sins, who helps us in times of trial and delivers us from evil.

So praying the Lord's Prayer is like singing in a choir or playing in a band directed by the one who wrote the music. Or it is like being coached by the one who invented the game and who will judge the outcome. Or it is like being given the answers by the one who will give you the test. Jesus, the one who bears our prayers and answers them, puts the words into our mouths to teach us to pray.

But God doesn't even stop there. "We do not know how to pray as we ought," Paul says in Romans 8:26. Even when Jesus puts the words in our mouths, our prayers easily become routine and meaningless. We worry and doubt, wondering if God really listens. Or we start thinking about how sincere we are and how God must be impressed with how much we want help. No matter how hard we try, we can't pray as we should.

But God isn't waiting for us to make our prayers good

Jim Whitmer

enough. Having said that we may pray, having commanded us to pray, and having taught us to pray, God prays with and for us. The "Spirit intercedes with sighs too deep for words" Paul says (Romans 8:26). It's like a father or mother who helps a child in every way and finally says, "Here, I'll do that for you." Having said to each of us, "You are mine," God goes all the way for us, even praying for us.

That's the basis for our confidence, and that's why we can pray with complete certainty that God hears us. We can pray to God as children speak to their loving parents, confidently and joyfully, because God promises that we may, commands us and teaches us to pray, and then prays with and for us.

119

Calling God Father

That's why we can call God *Father*, calling out to him as you call out to your mother or father at home: "Dad" or "Mom." God became your Father when you were baptized, when God first promised to be your God. That was and is God's promise to you. Not, "I'm going to be like a father," or "like a mother to you," but "I'm going to be your God"—your father and mother all wrapped up into one.

We can call God *Father*, too, because he is going to dwell with us, as the book of Revelation says (21:3). He isn't an absentee father who stays away, sending home occasional letters and gifts. God dwells with us now, in the Word and the sacraments. And God will stay with us in the future, raising us from the dead to take us to be with Christ. Then we will live with God as loving parents live with their children.

The old self doesn't care for this. In fact, it hates this. Prayer is a big problem for the old sinner in us, something to be avoided or used only for your own purposes, because when you pray you are admitting that you need God's help and grace. That's the one thing the old Adam or Eve doesn't want to admit, not unless it's with the provision that you can tell God exactly what to do and how to do it. So the old you makes the Lord's Prayer automatic and pointless or else insists that God has to do your bidding.

But once you hear the promise in and behind it, the Lord's Prayer becomes entirely different. Putting the old Adam or Eve to death in each of us, God calls out the new you—the you who can and will call on God with joy and certainty. As this new you comes forth, the you who is a believer, the Lord's Prayer blossoms and sings with all the love and grace of God's promise.

Then it's not dead repetition or some kind of hocus-pocus anymore, something that we just do out of habit. Rather, it is a person-to-person conversation with your God, the God of the promise, the God of Good Friday and Easter. Then, boldly and confidently, you can begin by saying "Our Father in heaven" and when you have finished praying, say "Amen"—that's the way it's going to be.

18
PRAYING FOR OUR FATHER

THE FIRST PETITION

Hallowed be your name.

What does this mean?

God's name certainly is holy in itself, but we ask in this prayer that we may keep it holy.

When does this happen?

God's name is hallowed whenever his Word is taught in its truth and purity and we as children of God live in harmony with it. Help us to do this, heavenly Father! But anyone who teaches or lives contrary to the Word of God dishonors God's name among us. Keep us from doing this, heavenly Father!

THE SECOND PETITION

Your kingdom come.

What does this mean?

God's kingdom comes indeed without our praying for it, but we ask in this prayer that it may come also to us.

God's kingdom comes when our heavenly Father gives us his Holy Spirit, so that by his grace we believe his holy Word and live a godly life on earth now and in heaven forever.

One of the biggest surprises in the Lord's Prayer comes right at the beginning. In the first three petitions—the two above plus the one that will be considered in the next chapter—Jesus teaches us to pray *for* God. The last four petitions are more like what we would expect; in them we pray *to* God for our neighbors and ourselves.

In the first petitions, then, we're not only praying *to* God but *for* God—that God's name will be hallowed and that God's kingdom will come. Why?

There could be one easy explanation. If these petitions hadn't been taught to us by Jesus, someone could say that we're trying to butter God up a little bit, saying a few nice words about God's name and the new day before getting down to what's really important, what we want or need.

But that's not the way the God of the promise—the God of the Exodus, Good Friday, and Easter—operates. Not for a minute. God is no pompous, swelled head who keeps one hand on the treasure chest while holding out the other to be stroked with bribes. God is the God who promises, the God who raised Jesus from the dead, your heavenly Father who gives all things by grace, as a gift, without payment or price.

Why do we pray for God, then? Maybe if we look at what we're asking for, we'll get some clues. Then we'll come back to this question and see if we can't find an answer.

God's name and goal

The Introduction to the Lord's Prayer and the First Petition go together just like the first two commandments. In the Commandments, after promising to be our God and giving us the name, God commands us to use the name rightly. The beginning of the Lord's Prayer follows the same order. After calling upon God as our Father in the Introduction, we pray in the First Petition that God's name will be hallowed.

Now *hallowed* or *holy* isn't a common word. The Lord's Prayer is probably the only place where you use it regularly. But if you take the Second Commandment as a clue, you should have a pretty good idea of what it means. When we pray "Hallowed be your name," we are asking God to give us what is commanded in the Second Commandment. We are asking that God will bring out the new you in us who will use God's name as God intends it to be used, to "call upon him in prayer, praise, and thanksgiving."

Jim Whitmer

That's just the opposite of what the old self wants. The old you in you is always wondering how you can make a name for yourself, a name people will respect, admire, and appreciate. To this old you, God's name is good for nothing. It is a name to be used to curse and swear, to lie and deceive, to conjure up magic, or to prove how religious you are. The old self's contempt for God's name is so deep and so wide that there is almost nothing more common than taking his name in vain.

As the new you that God calls out in Baptism takes shape, however, something different happens. Instead of using it as an exclamation point for curses and lies, the new you takes God's name as a great and precious gift. Because God has given you his name, you can call upon God, asking for help, praising God, and giving thanks for all of the promises and gifts God has given. You know who God is, what kind of a God you have. Your God is the one who makes things out of nothing and raises the dead, the God of grace who speaks to you through his word to make you and all things new.

Hearing that, something else happens to the new you, too. Instead of being embarrassed or slightly ashamed to use God's name, the new you treats it as the name that is above every other name. It is the name to speak to others, telling all who will listen what God has done and promises to do. That's another way God intends his name to be used: so that we can give the word of grace to others.

The old self knows how to speak of God to others, too. When it goes religious, the old sinner in us makes the clouds echo with shouts of "Praise God," "Praise the Lord," and so on. But somehow when the old self gets hold of the name, it always gets turned around to point to himself or herself. "Praise God" on the old self's lips means "Praise me, for I am so religious." "Praise the Lord" means "Look at me, and you'll see the genuine article."

The name properly used

So when we pray "Hallowed be your name," we're not only asking God to continue making a new you in us who will use the name properly, we're asking God to see to it that his name is used properly wherever it is spoken. God's name is hallowed or holy, then, "wherever his Word is taught in its truth and purity and we as children of God live in harmony with it." God's going to make that happen, calling out the new you in us and a new creation across the face of the universe that will see the good in God's name and use it accordingly.

The Second Petition, "Your kingdom come," fits in with the Commandments, too. In the Third Commandment, God commands us to remember the day—not only the Sabbath day each week but the new day coming. In this petition, we pray for the new day, asking that God's kingdom will come.

The word *kingdom* probably isn't a part of your everyday language, either. It smacks of another age, the time of Robin Hood or Prince Valiant, when there were kings and lords who ruled over little kingdoms of their own.

God's kingdom isn't a place, as those were. God's kingdom is wherever God rules or reigns. God's kingdom comes wherever God takes charge. It will finally come when God takes control of all the earth and makes all things new.

God has taken charge of you already. God started in your Baptism, when God sent the Spirit to begin making the new you in you. The Spirit has been at work since—calling you, gathering you with others, enlight-

Marilyn Nolt

ening you, sanctifying you.

But God's kingdom hasn't come finally, yet. God has a rival in you, the old you. And though they are not nearly as powerful as he is, God has other rivals as well, "rulers and authorities" as they are called in Ephesians 6:12. When God's kingdom finally comes, God will destroy all of his rivals. Then there will be no more old Adam or Eve in you that fights and struggles against the new you. You will be wholly and completely God's. And then there will be no more rivals who fill the earth with sin and death. The creation will be new—God's own creation, the new creation.

So, in the Second Petition, we are praying for the new you and the new day. When we pray, "Your kingdom come," we are asking God to continue to take charge of us and to keep the promise, bringing in his rule or reign over all the earth. That is God's goal: to make us and all things new. And that's what God is going to do.

Jim Whitmer

126

Praying for God

Have you seen enough clues now to answer that first question, why Jesus teaches us to pray *for* God?

The first clue is in Luther's explanations to these petitions. We're not praying for God because God somehow needs help, ours or anyone else's. "God's name certainly is holy in itself"— God doesn't need our prayers or our help to make it holy. "God's kingdom comes indeed without our praying for it"— God doesn't have to wait for us to pray in order to take control of things.

"All right," the old you says, "if that's the case, why bother to pray these petitions at all? If God can get along without me, why should I bother my head about God's name and kingdom?" The old Adam or Eve always likes to make it sound as if it is doing God a favor. It's the old you who thinks you can "allow" God to do something, as if God were some helpless person who had to come and ask for your permission before doing what God wants.

That's not the way it works. God doesn't need permission from us for anything. God doesn't need our prayers or occasional good deeds, either. God doesn't depend on us—we depend on God.

Why do we pray these petitions, then? In both of these petitions, while we are praying for God, we are also praying for ourselves, that God's name will be holy among us and that God's kingdom will come to us.

Does that sound complicated? Think of your school's basketball or hockey team. If you don't play for the team, there's nothing you can do to help them win. When the whistle blows, all you can do is sit and watch or stand and cheer.

But still you hope, and maybe pray, too, that your team will have a good game. And you hope and maybe even pray, too, that they will "establish their rule" over all the other teams, defeating every rival and taking home the championship.

If they win their games and get a good reputation, the team members get some benefits for themselves. But you benefit from it, too. Otherwise you wouldn't feel bad if they lost.

Now, God doesn't hold pep meetings or organize cheering sections with pastors for cheerleaders. Furthermore, there's no doubt about who will win the game. God's going to win it, hands down.

But still we pray, as Jesus taught us to pray, "Hallowed be your name," and "Your kingdom come." We pray for God because we love God and want God's name to be used as God intends it to be used and because we want God to take control of all things. But while we pray for God, we are also praying for ourselves. We ask that God will help us to use the name as God intends it to be used—that God will hear our prayers and keep giving us the Word. And we ask that God will keep reaching into our hearts, taking hold of us by grace so that we can live as people of faith.

19
VICTORY IS CERTAIN

THE THIRD PETITION

Your will be done, on earth as it is in heaven.

What does this mean?

The good and gracious will of God is surely done without our prayer, but we ask in this prayer that it may be done also among us.

When does this happen?

God's will is done when he hinders and defeats every evil scheme and purpose of the devil, the world, and our sinful self, which would prevent us from keeping his name holy and would oppose the coming of his kingdom. And his will is done when he strengthens our faith and keeps us firm in his Word as long as we live. This is his gracious and good will.

There are two sides to this petition, just as there are two sides to every person's story, including your own. On the one side this petition is full of certainty: "The good and gracious will of God is surely done without our prayer." Because God is God, God is going to take control, no matter what.

But then there's the other side: "But we ask in this prayer that it may be done also among us." Is that for certain, too? Sometimes it doesn't seem very certain at all. For wherever God's Word and promise are heard, there is bound to be opposition and plenty of it.

Maybe you've seen the same two sides in your own story. On the one side, God has made a decision about you, promising to be your God and to give you everything good. You have received all kinds of gifts from God, too. This is certain.

But on the other side, maybe you haven't been able to see good in everything that has happened to you. Maybe you have had some times of uncertainty and doubt about God's promises or about yourself. Maybe, after looking around, you've seen some things that make you wonder who is really in charge in the world—if it's God or some unknown, unseen power that rules by chance and luck. Maybe, in fact, you've sometimes wondered if this whole business about God and the promise isn't just talk, a nice idea that sounds good but doesn't really mean much.

Jean-Claude Lejeune

These two sides to your own story and the stories of all God's people are the special concern of the Third Petition. As we pray "Your will be done, on earth as in heaven," we are asking God to put the two sides together—to give us the certainty of the promise in the midst of the opposition, pain, and trouble that we know.

So in this chapter, we'll consider two things: first, the other side of the story, some of the opposition we see; and second, what God does with this opposition.

The opponents

Sometimes it seems that living in God's promises ought to be like cruising down a freeway through the wide open spaces on a beautiful summer afternoon. If it were, you wouldn't have to worry about anything like traffic, fog, intersections, possible accidents, or breakdowns along the way.

But that's not the way it works, not if what happened to Jesus, Peter, Paul, the prophets before them, and Christians since is any indication. Wherever the gospel goes, it makes people new, giving freedom from the past and hope for the future. But wherever it goes it also meets opposition. In fact, the more the gospel is proclaimed and heard, the more it is fought.

You know what happened to Jesus. If anyone could have expected a cruising, easy time, it should have been Jesus. He was and is God's own beloved Son, after all.

But there were two sides to his story, too. As he proclaimed God's promise and went to work with it, some heard and believed. But others, including his own disciples, doubted. And still others met him with the most fearsome opposition, until finally he was crucified.

"Remember the word that I said to you," Jesus told his disciples when he was leaving them, " 'Servants are not greater than their master.' If they persecuted me, they will persecute you" (John 15:20). "In the world you face persecution," he said (John 16:33). That's the way it works. Just as Jesus met a ready welcome from some and was condemned by others, today his word is heard by some and opposed by others.

Who are these opponents? Luther lists three of them. They are our sinful self, the world, and the devil.

By now you are familiar with the first opponent. "Our sinful self" is the old you, the old Adam or Eve in you and each of us. While piously praying "Your will be done," the old self's deepest wish is just the opposite: "My will be done." That's where the conflict centers. Whenever you hear God's Word and promise, the old you fights it. And it continues to fight it as long as you live, no matter how hard you struggle against the sinner in you.

The old self tries to make it look as if you're in charge of things while God is some kind of super servant who takes your orders. To this end, the old sinner in us plots and schemes, sometimes coming straight out with unbelief or indifference to the promise, at other times trying to make you look religious while holding out for your own way.

The second opponent is familiar to you, too. It is the world. You're not the only one with an old self in you. All of us have this old you in us—every living human being. So we don't just resist the promises of God alone. We have a world of company.

The world's creed has three articles: good luck, hard work, and getting ahead. In the first article the world insists that everything happens by luck. If you get something you've wanted, it's because you're lucky. If you don't, you're unlucky.

But sometimes it takes more than luck. So the world's creed has a second article: hard work. If people will only knuckle down and put their minds to it, the world says, they'll be able to do whatever they want.

The third article is the goal: getting ahead, ahead of what you've gotten so far, ahead of your neighbors, ahead of whoever gets in your way.

So the world resists the gospel. It is too busy looking for luck, working hard, and getting ahead to have any time for promises. Either that or it wants promises that work like coupons—you turn them in someplace and get ahead some more. It's not a joke—perhaps you've tasted some of the ridicule that sometimes comes from other people when they hear you have ears for the promise. That's just the beginning.

The third opponent of the gospel is the devil. To the old sinner in us and the world, the suggestion that there might actually be a devil seems ridiculous. Because the old self keeps insisting that you can take charge of everything that happens to you, it doesn't want you thinking that there is anything like a powerful force of evil around that might be stronger than you are.

People who have wrestled with the promise know something different, though: No matter how hard we struggle, hope, and pray for faith, something stronger than us seems to be fighting against us. That's the devil's speciality.

Luther used to call the devil "God's ape," God's mimic. The devil makes itself look like God, imitating God to destroy faith. So wherever the devil goes, it leaves footprints full of doubt, despair, anxiety, and agony. Either that or it lulls people to sleep with its imitations, making them imagine that they are secure and need not be bothered with God's promise.

Though they are nowhere near as powerful as God is, with three opponents like these hard at work it's no wonder the world is so full of pain, struggle, and death. It's not surprising either that God's opponents would like to pin the blame on God for the suffering they cause in the creation.

Hindering and strengthening

What do you suppose God does with these opponents? You can be sure that God is not going to sit in heaven twiddling cosmic thumbs. God's will is to bring out the new you in us and to bring in the new creation, God's kingdom. So God fights the opponents of the promise in two ways: God "hinders and defeats every evil scheme and purpose" they come with, and God "strengthens our faith and keeps us firm in his Word as long as we live."

God uses several means to hinder and defeat the old self and its partners. First of all, God uses the Commandments to pen them up or keep them on leashes, putting them under controls that keep them from going too far. In this way, God keeps order in the creation and protects each of us.

Then, while keeping order, God takes away the opponents' weapons and turns them around against the enemies. For instance, one of the devil's favorite weapons is death. The devil will wave it in front of you saying, "What difference does it

133

make? You're going to die anyway," and so try to frighten you into thinking that nothing matters but trying to grab as much as you can while you can.

But then God takes hold of the weapon the devil is using and turns it on the devil: "Yes," God says to you, "you are going to die. It's not going to be any fun, either. But here is my promise: I am going to raise you from the dead."

In this way, God uses the fright and worry the devil has caused in you to show you how great and gracious the promises are. Luther called this God's "strange work." What the sinful self, the world, and the devil use to drive you from the promise—such as suffering, pain, and death—God uses to drive you to the promise.

But God doesn't just fight the opponents from a distance. In Christ, God has taken them upon himself, doing battle with his enemies to bring them to their knees and put them to death. Now they die each time that you hear Christ's word and promise. On the last day, God will put them to death forever. That's the goal that God has set for us and the whole creation: to destroy all of his enemies and make all things new.

In the meantime, while God hinders and defeats these enemies, God also encourages us by strengthening our faith and keeping us firm in the Word. God does this through the Spirit, who works in the Word and the sacraments. Day after day the Spirit speaks to us, telling us all that God has done and will do to make us Christ's own.

Having given us the word of our Baptism, that God will be our God, God also comes to be with us in the Lord's Supper, renewing us, strengthening us, giving us hope and courage. Through it all, God surrounds us with other people who will help and care for us. God works to keep us in faith.

There are two sides to your story, just as there are two sides to Jesus' story and two sides to everyone's story. So we all pray, "Your will be done, on earth as in heaven," asking that God will give us the certainty that his will "may be done also among us." God will give us that certainty because God is God, and God never breaks a promise.

20
EVERY DAY A GIFT

THE FOURTH PETITION
Give us today our daily bread.

What does this mean?

God gives daily bread, even without our prayer, to all people, though sinful, but we ask in this prayer that he will help us to realize this and to receive our daily bread with thanks.

What is meant by "daily bread"?

Daily bread includes everything needed for this life, such as food and clothing, home and property, work and income, a devoted family, an orderly community, good government, favorable weather, peace and health, a good name, and true friends and neighbors.

THE FIFTH PETITION

Forgive us our sins as we forgive those who sin against us.

What does this mean?

We ask in this prayer that our Father in heaven would not hold our sins against us and because of them refuse to hear our prayer. And we pray that he would give us everything by grace, for we sin every day and deserve nothing but punishment. So we on our part will heartily forgive and gladly do good to those who sin against us.

After praying for the great and glorious gifts of God—God's name, kingdom, and will—now we get down to the basic stuff of daily life: bread and butter and getting along with our neighbors.

To be sure, the first three petitions have plenty to do with daily life, too. As God creates the new you in us who will keep God's name holy, God charges our days with freedom. And as God helps us to look forward to the coming of the kingdom, God fills our days with hope, giving us the whole new creation to look forward to.

But freedom and hope for the new day wouldn't be complete if our tables were empty or if we had to wonder constantly what God and our neighbors think of us. So, after teaching us to pray for the new you and the new creation, Jesus tells us to ask for daily bread and forgiveness, as well.

It's not that we somehow have to talk God into giving us these gifts. Most all of us have enough daily bread already, many more than their share. And over and over again, God has assured us of forgiveness. God will continue to give us these gifts, along with everything else we need to live while we await the new day. That's the promise—the promise of the First Commandment and all three articles of the Creed.

The trouble is that we don't always realize it. In fact, we seldom do. We either take daily bread and forgiveness for granted, never giving them a thought, or we worry ourselves sick about them, thinking that somehow God will forget us. So Jesus teaches us to pray for these gifts, helping us in this way to realize who gives them to us.

Why is it so hard to realize that these are gifts? That's the first question we'll consider in this chapter. After that, we'll discuss what realizing the gifts can mean for daily life.

Looking to ourselves

If there's one thing your neighbors have in common with you, it is worrying. They might be taller or shorter, fatter or skinnier; they might be neighbors across the street, across the border, or across the ocean, but you can be sure that they worry just like you do. Worrying seems to be one common denominator that marks us all as people.

Sometimes there seems to be very good reason for worry. To put bread on our tables, for instance, it takes a whole combination of people and things working together. It takes good farmers, good farms, good crops, good prices, good stores, and good jobs to earn good money.

Food isn't all we need to live each day, either. We also need clothing, places to live, good governments to protect us, good names, and good neighbors, plus more. And each requires its own combination of people and things working together.

With so many needs and so many combinations needed to get them, it isn't any wonder that people worry. You may not have gone to bed hungry once in your life. But many people do and with the sinful self, the world, and the devil hard at work, there's no guarantee that you won't sometime be one of them. That can be worrisome.

If you haven't yet had to worry about the food on your table or the other things you need for your body, you may have sometimes wondered—possibly even worried—about what other people think of you. That, too, seems to be one of our characteristics as people: feeling out of step or out of place with the people around us. Some notice it more, some less, but the feeling always seem to be there somewhere, gnawing its way around.

Here again there may seem to be good reason for it. You might have done something that makes you feel guilty. Or you might just feel there is something about you that makes you less than acceptable, less than desirable, whether it's as small as an unsightly wart or as big as feeling awkward, ugly, or stupid.

If that isn't enough, there can be some deeper worries. No matter how often we hear God's promise of forgiveness, at times it is easy to become convinced that we have done things to disqualify ourselves from it, that we're out of place or out of step not only with some neighbors, but with God. At such times, people can try as hard as they want to not to worry about it, but the feeling keeps coming back.

It is these worries about what we need to live and what others think of us that make it so difficult to realize that God gives us everything we need as a gift. They are the old you's worries. That's how the sinful self, the world, and the devil work—by focusing our attention on what we love or fear and making it appear that we have to get or avoid those things by ourselves. Then we worry.

See how it works? As long as we're worried, we keep looking to ourselves, trying to find ways to get what we want or to avoid what we fear. Then if we get enough food and get along well with others, we take such gifts for granted and start worrying about something else we want or fear. Or if we're hungry and feeling guilty, we concentrate on how hungry and guilty we are. No matter which way it goes, God's Word and promise are ignored and forgotten.

Worries, whether well based or imaginary, always come from God's opponents. They are the only gifts they can give us, and they give us as much as they can, trying to convince us that we should always look to ourselves and ourselves alone. Then worries become a circle, one worry feeding on another and another until the circle closes in with no apparent escape. Soon the promise is forgotten altogether.

Looking to the promise

How's this circle going to be broken? Well, one thing's sure from the beginning: It's not going to be broken as long as we keep looking to ourselves. If you've ever had a bad attack of worries, you know that. It doesn't do a bit of good to say "Don't worry" or "There's nothing to be afraid of" at such a time. Hearing such words, you just worry about being worried or get scared of being scared.

No, it takes a different kind of looking entirely, a looking away from ourselves to the promise. That's what the Spirit does: The Holy Spirit turns our eyes from ourselves to the God who has decided for us and to the promises God has made.

This God doesn't just say, "Don't worry," and then go away, leaving us in our fears. This God says, "I promise to be your God and give you everything good." And then God keeps his word, giving us not only daily bread, but the other things we need to live from day to day.

God doesn't just say, "Don't feel guilty," or "Don't be ashamed," either. God says, "Here's what I've done about your guilt. I have heaped it all on Christ and he's carried it for you, drowning all your sins and guilt in my grace." Or God says, "Here's what I think of you, with all of your shame: I love you more than you could love or hate yourself. You are mine."

God goes even further, speaking the Word day after day; God comes to you to be with you and each of us in the Sacrament of the Lord's Supper, reassuring us again with the Word and the bread and wine that he will never let us down.

When you look to this promise, then, realizing that all of God's gifts are for you, everything changes. You don't have to look to yourself for your daily bread and the other things you need to live each day. You don't have to pretend that you must

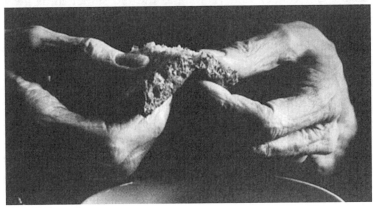

J. Michael Fitzgerald

earn everything, worrying night and day about how you can get and grab some more.

Hearing this promise, you can receive all that God gives you for what they are: gifts. And you can count on the God who raised Jesus from the dead to give you all you need. Then, when you see your daily bread as a gift, you can share it with others, passing on the gifts to other people who haven't received as much as you have.

The same thing happens with the word of forgiveness. When God says to you, "In my name all your sins are forgiven," you don't have to worry about what God thinks of you. God has told you that nothing will be held against you. You don't have to prove yourself to God, trying to whip up enough sincerity or goose bumps to show you deserve it. "I don't care whether you deserve it or not," God says, "you're mine—insincerity, doubts, guilt, shame, and all."

When God forgives you so freely, you can do the same with your neighbors. That's why Jesus put the Fifth Petition together the way it is: "Forgive us our sins as we forgive those who sin against us." Jesus isn't trying to make a deal with us. The God who promises doesn't make deals. God forgives us our failures to forgive, too. But as God forgives us, God intends the forgiveness to go through us to our neighbors. As that happens, it's a sure sign that the Spirit is at work, forgiving us as promised.

Realizing that God gives us all that we need as gifts makes all the difference, then. As long as the old sinner in us gives us eyes only for ourselves, our worries become whirlpools, pulling us in deeper and deeper until finally it seems we'll drown in anxiety. The old self has good reason to worry: God is putting that self in you to death.

But as the Spirit gives us ears and eyes for the promise, calling out the new you who looks to the promise, each day becomes a gift. We can then pray for our daily bread and ask God to forgive us our sins as we forgive others in the certainty that God will hear us and give us these gifts, as he has promised.

That's freedom—freedom from the old self's worry, guilt, and shame; freedom for the joyful service of God's people. There's no other freedom like it. God's promise makes every day new.

140

21
DELIVERANCE

THE SIXTH PETITION

Save us from the time of trial.

What does this mean?

God tempts no one to sin, but we ask in this prayer that God would watch over us and keep us so that the devil, the world, and our sinful self may not deceive us and draw us into false belief, despair, and other great and shameful sins. And we pray that even though we are so tempted we may still win the final victory.

THE SEVENTH PETITION

And deliver us from evil.

What does this mean?

We ask in this inclusive prayer that our heavenly Father would save us from every evil to body and soul, and at our last hour would mercifully take us from the troubles of this world to himself in heaven.

The key to just about any good play in football, hockey, or basketball is the fake—making it seem as if you're going to do one thing when actually you're planning to do something else. When they work, fakes throw the defense off guard, opening up weaknesses that enable the offense to score or move closer to it.

There is nothing fake about temptations. They are terribly real. But they can be awfully deceptive, too. The less dangerous ones—temptations to curse, lust, steal, or lie—can look the most powerful. And the most dangerous temptations, like false belief and despair, can look weak and harmless. While you're setting up a defense against the temptations you see most clearly, the more dangerous ones come along from the other direction, hitting you blind side to rob you of the freedom and hope of the promise.

Luther sometimes called the smaller temptations "puppy sins." It's not that they aren't difficult or harmful. It's just that they are weak in comparison to the big ones, which always come silently or secretly to attack God's word for us.

Jesus has given us the Sixth and Seventh Petitions for both kinds of temptation. But he is especially concerned with the big ones. So in the Sixth Petition, "Save us from the time of trial," he teaches us to ask God for help with our temptations now, to keep us in faith while we await the new day. And in the Seventh, the concluding petition, he teaches us to pray also for the last day, when God will remove us from all temptations and every evil to take us to himself.

That leaves us with a couple of questions. First, what are these temptations that are so powerful? And second, how does God help us with them?

The hidden tempters

Something strange happens as God makes the new you. You might expect that this new you would get stronger and stronger until finally you wouldn't be tempted at all. That's partially true; the new you does get stronger in the promise.

But with temptation, it's just the opposite. The more you hear and want God's promise, the stronger the temptations get. It's like learning to drive—the more you learn, the more aware you become of the dangers.

That's how the big temptations work; they are sneaky, silent, and deadly. Their target is the promise of the First Commandment, God's promise, given to us in Christ, to be our God. Two of these big temptations are listed in Luther's explanation: false belief and despair.

To start with, false belief might not seem like much of a temptation, not nearly as tempting as gossiping or coveting. What does it matter what people believe, after all? Isn't it a free country?

That's the fake—false belief looks harmless at first. But what is false belief? Since God's decision to be our God in Christ,

Richard West

forgiving us and adopting us, is the most important belief we have, false belief is something that denies this promise.

False beliefs works in just this way. All of them say, in one way or another, that God's decision isn't enough or good enough for us. So, either they say that we ourselves have to do what God has promised to do, or they say that God goes part way and we go the rest of the way in response. The God of the promise is treated like a liar, then, and you lose the freedom and hope of the promise.

Do you find that tempting? Probably not, when it's put that way. But the old Adam or Eve is the master of disguise. It puts much nicer clothing on it to make it more attractive.

"It doesn't matter what you believe as long as you're sincere," the old sinner in us will say, as if God had never spoken a word and we could make up anything we want about God. If that doesn't work, the old self will flip the coin so it comes down on the other side, making the promise into a law. "Now you have to believe this," it will say, "and believe it just as I tell it to you. Otherwise, there is no hope for you." The sinner makes God's Word out to be something so stupid that we have to be forced to accept it. Either way, the hope and joy of the promise is denied.

The second powerful temptation Luther lists in his explanation of the Sixth Petition is despair. Again, that doesn't sound like much of a temptation. But when things start to go wrong, when nothing seems to go the way you hope it will, it seems only natural to get discouraged, to lose heart.

It's not surprising that things go bad sometimes. Even though God controls those three opponents—the devil, the world, and our own flesh—they can still do enough damage to make us feel helpless and hopeless.

That's what makes despair such a sneaky temptation. It begins so quietly, in such a subtle way. And that's what makes it so difficult to fight, too. Like worries and guilt, hopelessness feeds on itself, pulling us down into despair until finally there seems to be no way out. And then, fight though we may, God's Word and promise don't seem true or helpful for us. The freedom and hope God promises to us in the Word are lost for us, covered by the old self's hopelessness.

144

Jean-Claude Lejeune

So we pray, "Save us from the time of trial," asking that God will watch over us so that we don't get lured into such things as false belief and despair. Praying this petition, we are asking God to protect us now from anything that would lead us away from the promise.

Power in weakness

The apostle Paul tells a story in 2 Corinthians 12 that shows how God helps us in temptation. Paul says that he had a "thorn in the flesh," something that bothered him deeply. "Three times I appealed to the Lord about this," he says, "that it would leave me, but he said to me, 'My grace is sufficient for you, for power is made perfect in weakness'" (verses 8-9).

That's another puzzling answer, isn't it? God refused to take away whatever it was that bothered Paul. But still God gave Paul all that Paul could ask for and more: God's grace.

145

That's how God helps us. Now, while we wait for the new day, God doesn't take us out of temptation, somehow making us immune to it or exempt from it. God is going to keep us here, where there is temptation, because this is where our jobs are.

But if God doesn't take us out of temptation, God gives us what Paul also received: grace that never ends, gifts on top of gifts, enabling us to live in temptation with faith and our hopes up. "My grace is sufficient for you," God says, "for *you*." It is the grace of God's promise to be your God, God's decision to make the new you who will be what God created you to be— a believer. It is the grace of God's promise to take you as you are, putting the old self to death in you and promising to raise you from the dead. It is the grace that comes to you in the Word and sacraments, assuring you and reassuring you that whatever happens, Christ is yours and you are Christ's.

Jean-Claude Lejeune

That's how Jesus fought the tempter—with God's Word and promise of grace. When Jesus was led into the wilderness to be tempted, he didn't rely on his own strength or power, as he very well could have. Instead, each time the devil came Jesus met him with the Word. "It is written," Jesus said, " 'One does not live by bread alone, but by every word that comes from the mouth of God' " (Matthew 4:4).

The Word is the power God gives us in our weakness. We shall be tempted right up to our last day and hour. If it weren't for God's promise of grace, we would be beaten by temptations right up to the last hour, too. But God has filled our ears with the Word, encouraging us, comforting us, upholding us, and uplifting us. God's Word is God's power, the power of the Spirit to uphold us in our weakness, to overcome all the temptations we face, to win the victory for us.

But that's not the end of the story. At our last hour, when the last day comes, God is going to deliver us from all evil—anything and everything that threatens us in any way. God is going to destroy all the old enemies—the sinful self, the rebellious world, and the devil—making us and the creation completely new.

Who is going to do that? Your creator, the one who in Christ, taught you this prayer. For this God is the God of the promise, the God who raised Jesus from the dead, the God who will raise you from the dead. "See, I am making all things new," God says (Revelation 21:5). "Amen," we say. That's the way it's going to be.

THE MEANS OF GRACE

22
HOW DO YOU KNOW?

To obtain such faith God instituted the office of the ministry, that is, provided the Gospel and the sacraments. Through these, as through means, he gives the Holy Spirit, who works faith, when and where he pleases, in those who hear the Gospel.

Augsburg Confession Article V

A big question has lurked behind the Commandments, the Creed, and the Lord's Prayer, ready to throw all they say into doubt. It has come up in our discussions a few times. The question is "How do you know?"

Sometimes it can be the old sinner's question. When it asks, "How do you know?" there is a sneer behind it. The old Adam or Eve has all the answers already.

But this question can be asked in another way, too. It can come to each of us, not because we've made up our minds that there can't be an answer, but in the hope that somehow we can know, and know for certain, that God's decision and promise are meant for us.

What is the answer, then? How can we know that God's decision and promise are meant for each of us? Answer: Through the Word and the sacraments God gives us in the church.

That answer may sound familiar, but you may be surprised. Together, the Word and the sacraments are called the "means of grace." They are the vehicles God uses, the routes God takes, to give us gifts and to show us that the promises are for us. Through them, "he gives the Holy Spirit, who works faith," as the Augsburg Confession says. In them, God calls out, sustains, fosters, nurtures, strengthens, upholds, and uplifts the new you in us to give us the certainty of the promise.

Hidden in the Word

The first big surprise is the common things God uses for the means of grace. It could be expected that God would overwhelm us, coming with crowds of angels or lightning flashes of glory. But look at what God uses: words, water, bread, and wine. You could hardly find four more ordinary things.

Carlin Stock Photos

Words fill your day from morning to night; there is water just about everywhere; bread sits on practically every table; wine was the usual drink at meals in Bible times and is available almost anywhere. Yet God takes these ordinary things and uses them to assure us of the promise.

Gene Plaisted/The Crosiers

This is the surprising thing about God's Word, too. To speak to us, God makes the Word just like one of ours—a word that rolls around the tongue and takes off between the teeth and lips to shake eardrums.

How has God done this? In Christ, first of all; then in the Bible, which bears witness to Christ; and finally in the spoken Word, the Word you hear as your pastor and others bear witness to Christ.

God's Word, first and foremost, is Christ. Jesus not only spoke God's Word, he is God's Word—"In the beginning was the Word," John says in his gospel. "And the Word became flesh and lived among us, and we have seen his glory, the glory as of a father's only son, full of grace and truth" (1:1, 14).

In Christ, God became a person just like us, coming as close to us as our own flesh and blood. He was born just as we were; ate, slept, and struggled as we do; and talked in a language like our own. Jesus said it in word and deed; he took upon himself our sin and our death; he was raised from the dead for us. Christ is God's Word—he said it and did it for us.

God's Word also comes to us through the Bible. It, too, is common and ordinary in many ways. It is printed on paper with ink and bound in covers like any other book. And it tells of ordinary people, men and women who believe and doubt, who wonder how they can know for sure, who struggle and fight.

151

But Christ sets the Bible apart from other books. Jesus makes it holy; he makes the Bible God's Word. Because the Bible tells his story, from beginning to end, it is God's Word. Through it, God speaks to us, telling us all that he has said and done and will do in Christ.

The third way God speaks to us is another surprise, but one we've hinted at before. God speaks to us through preaching— the living witness of pastors and others as they bear witness to Christ.

God speaks to you through the voice of pastors because they name Christ to you, not because of any other quality they might possess. As preachers proclaim the Word to you, telling you of God's decision and promise to be your God, of Christ's death and resurrection, God is giving you the Word.

God speaks to you through other people, too. As your parents, guardians, grandparents, brothers, sisters, cousins, friends, or Sunday school teachers have told you of Christ, God has been speaking through them. You know for sure that they

Mimi Forsyth

are ordinary people, but that's how God speaks—through words like our words spoken by people who talk like we do.

This is God's Word, then, and this is how it comes to us. First, above all, and always, God's Word is Christ. The Bible is God's Word because it bears witness to Christ. And preaching and teaching are God's Word insofar as they also bear witness to Christ, telling of his promise.

The living Word

But that's not all there is to it. God's Word is living and active, a word that snaps and crackles with life, making things happen wherever it goes.

Not every word is like that. Some words are just words. They don't do anything to you. When somebody tells you it is a quarter past two in Hong Kong or that winters can be cold, it doesn't make much difference to you.

But other words are alive. If someone you had been day-dreaming about suddenly came up to you and said, "I love you," the words could set you on fire. Or if the strongest person in your neighborhood stopped you and said, "I'll fix you," the words would either bring up your fists or set your legs in motion. Words like these are powerful—they do things, making things happen in and to you.

This is how God's Word works. Only it is much more powerful. When God said, "Let there be light" (Genesis 1:3), there was light. When Jesus said "Stand up, take your mat and go to your home" (Mark 2:11), a man who had been unable to move a muscle jumped to his feet.

Sometimes, though, God's Word can seem so common and ordinary, so much like any other word, that it doesn't appear to do much. When you read the Bible, for instance, you might not always catch the promise in what is being said. Or when somebody starts explaining ideas about God, the ideas might sound okay but may never make you want to live or die for them.

Jesus didn't write books or give lectures explaining theories about God. He told all kinds of stories and parables to proclaim the promise. But Jesus always spoke the promise directly, person to person. "The kingdom of God has come near," he said.

"Repent, and believe in the good news" (Mark 1:15). "Blessed are the poor in spirit," he said, "for theirs is the kingdom of heaven" (Matthew 5:3). "I am the resurrection and the life. Those who believe in me, even though they die, will live, and everyone who lives and believes in me will never die," he said (John 11:25-26).

That's how God's Word is meant to come to you, also: as a promise, spoken to you by another person. God speaks commands to you, to keep the old self in line. But God has made the Word a common, ordinary, human word so that it can be spoken, so that you can hear it, so that it can be shouted, sung, whispered by one person to another. That's the whole purpose of the church: to bear the Word and speak it, to receive the sacraments and share them.

How can you know, then? How can you be sure? Listen. Open your ears. Somebody is going to say it to you: "God has promised to be your God, to give you everything good, to forgive your sin, to raise you from the dead." When you hear that, the words are going to do something to you.

The words may make you fight. You may doubt them, struggle with them, or take God's promise as too common or ordinary. But someday God is going to use the Word to make a believer out of you. Then you'll be sure, no matter how much you struggle. For it is God who speaks to you in this promise, God working through the Spirit to "work faith, when and where he pleases."

23
THE GREATEST MIRACLE

What is Baptism?

Baptism is not water only, but it is water used together with God's Word and by his command.

What is this Word?

In Matthew 28 our Lord Jesus Christ says: "Go therefore and make disciples of all nations, baptizing them in the name of the Father and of the Son and of the Holy Spirit."

If you are a miracle, your Baptism is a bigger one—the greatest of all. It looks so ordinary: some parents, some sponsors, and a pastor gathered around a bowl to say a few words and splash some water on a baby who either sleeps or screams, unaware of what's happening. Who'd ever guess there is anything earthshaking or miraculous about that?

But it's just like the God of the promise, to hide the most miraculous event in a simple ceremony. Baptism is a miracle greater than walking on water. For in it, with the washing of water and the pronouncement of his Word, God adopts each of us, takes us into the communion of saints, and gives us a future that not even death and the devil can destroy.

How do we know this? How do any of us know that God has done all this in our Baptism? That's the question we're going to consider in this chapter. For Baptism gives us the certainty that God's decision is for us. This certainty comes through the combination of water with the Word in God's command.

A *watery beginning*

In the last chapter we talked about the power in words. Some words are dead. They don't do anything to you or for you. But other words like "I love you" or "I'll get you" are alive. They make things happen, causing you to react in some way. Even simple words like "It's cold today" or "It's raining outside" have life in them. They make you put on gloves or wear a raincoat.

God's Word is the original lively word. It is so powerful that God told Jeremiah the Word is like a fire, "like a hammer that breaks a rock in pieces" (23:29). And God said to Isaiah, "So shall my word be that goes out from my mouth; it shall not return to me empty, but it shall accomplish that which I purpose, and succeed in the thing for which I sent it" (55:11). When God speaks his Word, it does what God says.

But when God's Word is spoken, other things can also happen. The words we speak aren't always so lively. Even words like "I love you" can lose their power and joy.

So when we hear God's Word spoken to us by someone else, it may not always be a lively, life-giving word that opens up the future for us. And sometimes, when it is spoken to all kinds of people, it can leave us wondering if this Word is really meant for us. For instance, when you hear Jesus' words from John 15:16, "You did not choose me but I chose you," you might wonder if Jesus has really chosen you, too.

That's why Christ has given us the sacraments. He wants to make sure that his Word and promise come home to us in a way we can't miss, as lively, life-giving words and promises that take hold of us, filling us with confidence in Christ. God wants to make sure there is no mistake about it, that each of us knows that the promises are meant precisely, exactly, and completely for us.

So in the sacraments, Christ puts his words together with some common, ordinary earthly things—water, bread, and wine—to give his gifts to us. This combination, Christ's giving us his Word with something earthly or physical, is what makes it a sacrament.

That's why Baptism is a watery beginning. In Baptism, Christ takes plain, ordinary water that has been drawn from a tap and puts it together with the Word to seal you as his own. It is as if Christ says, "Here now, with the washing of this water, you know that my Word and decision are for you. Now you can be certain, for I have washed you in my promise."

Mimi Forsyth

The Word in the wash

The old sinner's favorite attack on Baptism is to ignore the Word and concentrate on the water. "Water," it sniffs. "Water! Whoever heard of such a thing? You flush your toilets with water and now you say that God uses water to make you certain? Nonsense!"

157

If that doesn't work, the old Adam or Eve puts on some religion and tries to explain Baptism away. "Oh yes," the old you will say, "the water is a nice symbol. But what really counts is what you do with your Baptism. If you want to be sure of it, you have to make your Baptism complete by doing what God wants you to do."

Either way, whether by scorning the water or calling it a symbol, the old sinful self makes it sound as if Baptism is "water only." Then it can be ignored as a quaint ceremony for children or taken as something we have to do before getting down to what's really important: doing good things for Jesus. It's the same story. If the old self doesn't ignore the promise completely, it insists on trying to earn what God will only give as a gift.

Marilyn Nolt

But "Baptism is not water only," as Luther's explanation says. "It is water used together with God's Word. . . ." The water and the Word can't be separated, not without losing the sacrament. Apart from the Word, the water is plain, ordinary water. Apart from the water, the Word is still God's Word but the sacrament is gone. The Word and the water go together, the Word telling us what happens in the washing.

"Make disciples of all nations," Jesus said. How does this happen? By "baptizing them in the name of the Father and of the Son and of the Holy Spirit, and teaching them to obey everything that I have commanded you" (Matthew 28:19-20). This is Christ's Word, telling us what happens in the washing. As the Word is spoken, as the water is washed across our heads, Jesus makes us his disciples, his own beloved people.

So, in the speaking of the Word and the washing of the water, Christ gives birth to the new you in each of us, making us members of his church. Then, after our Baptism, he continues to be with us in the teaching of his Word and the Lord's Supper, sustaining and keeping the new you he has made. "And remember, I am with you always, to the end of the age," he says (Matthew 28:20).

That's why Baptism rings and sings with so much certainty. Where the old sinner in us can manage to separate the water from the Word, the certainty is lost. But when the Word and the water work together, as Christ promises they do, Baptism is more certain than the sunrise. For Christ himself is present in the Word, with the water, to make us his very own and give us all the gifts he has to give.

The loving command

There is one more essential ingredient in Baptism: Christ's command. "Go therefore," he says, "make disciples . . . baptizing them. . . ." That's an order.

Maybe it seems strange that Christ should command such a great and gracious gift. When Baptism is so full of grace, it's hard to understand why the whole world doesn't clamor for it, demanding to be baptized in his name.

But the truth is closer to the opposite. There is no gift, next to Christ himself, that the old Adam or Eve, the world, and the devil hold in deeper contempt. Baptism is the old self's funeral—the birth of the new you. So the old you attacks this sacrament with all the contempt, scorn, spite, malice, and hatred it can muster.

All of the old Adam's attacks on Baptism have the same purpose: to make it appear that it is something we do for God, not something God does for us. As a result, people wind up fearing, loving, and trusting in what they do, and Baptism finally doesn't matter. So unbelievers sneer at Baptism as a magic rite we do so we won't be afraid to die. Or the super pious ignore Baptism as if God can't do what he promises and concentrate on their own conversions, decisions for Christ, and experiences as far more important. Either way, Baptism is treated with contempt.

In all of these attacks, the fact that Christ commanded Baptism makes us all the more certain. It is a friendly command, a loving order Christ gives so that we will know how important Baptism is both to him and to us. Because he commanded it, we can be sure that Baptism is no human plaything—something invented by people to make us feel better. And we can be sure, too, that all of the old self's religious strutting about conversions and experiences is just that—strutting and nothing else.

Baptism is God's act for us. Though the pastor speaks the Word and does the washing, God is the one who baptizes. God is at work in every Baptism, putting the Word with the water to grace us. God keeps right on working, too, "to the end of the age" to be sure we're sure—to keep the new you in the certainty that is Christ's trademark.

24
OFF THE MERRY-GO-ROUND

What benefits does God give in Baptism?

In Baptism God forgives sin, delivers from death and the devil, and gives everlasting salvation to all who believe what he has promised.

What is God's promise?

In Mark 16 our Lord Jesus Christ says: "He who believes and is baptized will be saved; but he who does not believe will be condemned."

How can water do such great things?

It is not water that does these things, but God's Word with the water and our trust in this Word. Water by itself is only water, but with the Word of God it is a life-giving water which by grace gives the new birth through the Holy Spirit.

St. Paul writes in Titus 3: "He saved us . . . in virtue of his own mercy, by the washing of regeneration and renewal in the Holy Spirit, which he poured out upon us richly through Jesus Christ our Savior, so that we might be justified by his grace and become heirs in hope of eternal life. The saying is sure."

Your Baptism was a rehearsal of the last judgment. As the Word was spoken and the water washed across your head, God declared the verdict that will be pronounced over you when the last day comes. "Not guilty," God said. "This child is mine." Then, having rehearsed this verdict, God gave you all the gifts of the last judgment: forgiveness, deliverance, and everlasting salvation.

As the old sinner in us sees this promise, there has to be a catch somewhere. "How in the world can God do that?" it demands. "What's God trying to do? What does God want? We must have to do something!" So it hunts around, trying to find some kind of hidden agenda or concealed price tag to Baptism.

"Aha," the old you says, "here it is. We have to believe—that's the price tag. If you don't believe, you'll never get these gifts. It says so right in the Catechism, 'everlasting salvation to all who believe what he has promised,' 'he who believes and is baptized,' 'God's Word with the water and our trust in this Word.' That's what you have to do," the old self says, "now get busy and believe it."

There's method to the old self's madness. If it succeeds in convincing you that this is a condition you must meet if you are to receive God's promise, it will drive you into a circle that doesn't end. The chase will be on again.

God doesn't work that way, though. There is no catch, no trap, no hidden agenda or price tag to Baptism. It is a sheer gift, freely given. God wants you to believe that, and expects you to trust it is so. But God isn't waiting for you to come up with enough belief or trust on your own. God gives what God commands, making a believer out of you by putting the old you to death and raising up the new you with his gifts.

We'll look at the old Adam or Eve's endless circle first, and then consider how God gives us the faith to go with the promises.

The circle

Do you ever wonder what kind of impression you make on people? That seems to concern all of us at one time or another. And it can be painful, too, especially in regard to people who are important, whose impression of us matters.

The pain is in the wondering and doubting, as you try to figure out what people you admire really think of you. You might see some signs that they do respect you, that they're willing to be considered your friends. But then you might see some signs on the other side, too. They might not take time to talk with you, for instance, or you might not be invited along with them to something special. When that happens you can begin to feel rejected, left out, unliked, or unlikable.

What happens then? Well, you might decide that those people really weren't worth that much concern anyway, that you're better off without them. Or you might decide that you have to try harder, doing some things to make sure you make the kind of impression you want.

It might work to try harder. But it can turn out another way, too. If you try to make impressions, you can get caught on a merry-go-round where every effort to impress just makes you wonder and doubt all the more. You might buy some new clothes, for instance, and still wonder if they produce the right effect. You might try again by telling stories about your accomplishments. If that didn't work, you might try something different. Pretty soon you would be going in circles—trying, wondering, trying, wondering—never quite sure what the people you wanted to impress really thought of you.

When the old you succeeds in tying a condition to Baptism, making it appear that we have to show God how much we believe before God will give us the gifts, the same merry-go-round starts. We try to believe and then wonder if we've believed enough, try again and wonder some more, constantly working to come up with something that will put our doubts to rest.

It's like a story a pastor once told about her bishop. The man was glad he was humble, she said, because he knew that Christians should be humble. But then he was sad that he was glad that he was humble, because a person who is really humble shouldn't be glad about it. But then he was glad that he was sad that he was glad that he was humble, because at least when he was sad about being glad, he was humble again.

That's just how it works. When we start trying to manufacture our own faith, trying to drum up enough trust to show God

163

that we really deserve the promise, the merry-go-round keeps turning. We start putting faith in our faith, trusting our own trust, believing that we deserve the promise because we believe. That's not faith or trust in God and the promises, but faith in ourselves and what we've done or are doing. It's just one more of the old sinner's tricks.

The faith God gives

God doesn't send us on this kind of wild-goose chase. God doesn't expect us to believe by our own effort or strength. Rather, God gives us faith as a gift. God provides the belief and trust in us that go with the promises. How? In the Word, in Baptism, and in the Lord's Supper.

Look again at that concern for making good impressions. Some people make you feel that you have to do something special to impress them. But there are other people who let you know in small ways or large that they are already impressed with you, that they care for you and will accept you even when you don't feel very good about yourself.

Good friends are like that. You don't have to impress them. They're already impressed enough with you to like and respect you, even when you're at your worst. You can relax with them and be yourself without worrying what they think of you.

How do you learn to trust friends like that so completely? It's not by command. If somebody you didn't know came up to you and said, "Now you have to be my friend and trust me completely," you'd either ask why, excuse yourself politely, or turn around and run. No, you learn to trust close friends because they show you, in small ways and large, that they can be trusted.

That's how God gives us the faith that goes with the promises. In Baptism, God says, "Christ has given me my impression of you. In Christ, I have the best impression possible—the impression that you're not guilty, that you're one of mine and worth keeping forever. But that's not just my impression—it's my decision, word, and promise to you." Having said it, God acts on it, gracing you.

And that's just the beginning. From Baptism onward, God sends the Spirit to work in us day after day to make believers

Jim Whitmer

out of us. The Spirit moves in the Word, assuring us that God holds nothing against us and will not allow anything to come between us. The Spirit brings home the Word again and again to reassure us that having decided to be our God, God will raise us from the dead. All the while, the Spirit surrounds us with others in the church. The Holy Spirit is always at work to give us faith, to hold us and keep us in it. The Spirit is full of gifts, always giving.

That's just what the old self in us can't believe. "It can't be a gift," it says. "Somehow there has to be a catch to it. The world doesn't work that way. There's a catch to everything; you get what you pay for; you have to win friends and influence people. Think what would happen if God just gave these gifts. How would anyone ever be good if it weren't for a reward? And what about people who are baptized and never do anything about it? What about people who aren't baptized at all? There must be something we have to do ourselves to get what we want from God."

"No," God says, "there isn't a catch. All I have to give is yours, and I've given it to you in your Baptism, by grace alone. All I want is to make a believer out of you. And I'm doing that myself. I'm making you what I want you to be. I started in your Baptism, and I'm going to keep at it until the day I take you to myself."

Seeing that, recognizing and receiving the gift, is what finally destroys the old you. God's gifts are the death of it. For when you recognize the gift, you can see that all of the old self's attempts to impress God are worthless, just so much religious junk the old sinner in us puts on a display to show itself off. It is manufactured faith, sham religion, that is designed to impress God and others without asking too much of you. Finally, it can only drive you into the circle, putting you on the merry-go-round again.

But at the same time, when you recognize the gift, you can see how the new you is born in the water and the Word of Baptism. It is the you God is setting free. Knowing the promise of Baptism, you are free from having to impress God. You are free to call upon God, asking God to give you the belief and trust God promises to give. You are free from having to impress your neighbors. You are free to speak the Word to your neighbors, telling them of all God does and gives. You are free from having to wonder and doubt what the future and God's judgment will be. You are free to believe what God has already told you, tells you, and will keep telling you in the church: Those who believe and are baptized shall be saved. That's you. You can be sure of it.

25
LETTING GO TO TAKE HOLD

What does Baptism mean for daily living?

It means that our sinful self, with all its evil deeds and desires, should be drowned through daily repentance; and that day after day a new self, should arise to live with God in righteousness and purity forever.

St. Paul writes in Romans 6: "We were buried therefore with him by Baptism into death, so that as Christ was raised from the dead by the glory of the Father, we too might walk in newness of life."

Jesus once pictured repentance with a surprising parable. "The kingdom of heaven is like treasure hidden in a field," he said, "which someone found and hid; then in his joy he goes and sells all that he has and buys that field" (Matthew 13:44). Apparently the man wasn't even looking for a treasure—he just stumbled across it. And then, instead of advertising in the lost and found or telling the owner, he rushed out to find enough money to buy the field.

Both parts of the movement Jesus called repentance are in this story. First, because the treasure made the man willing to sacrifice everything he had for it. Then, he ran to buy the field, to take hold of the treasure.

Luther emphasizes both parts of the movement in his explanation of what Baptism means for daily living. As God gives his gifts, the sinful self dies each day and a new self, the new you, arises, getting wrapped up in the promise. We'll look at how this happens.

The drowning

With vaults and Swiss bank accounts available, the days when robbers—or crooked politicians—left buried treasures behind them are long gone.

But you may have found a treasure in another way and gone through the same kind of a movement the man in the parable did. Maybe, for instance, you've discovered that you are a much better student or athlete than you once thought. Or maybe you've found that you have some special talent—for music, mechanics, or something else—you didn't realize you had but that has now become very important to you.

If something like this has happened, you've experienced the first side of this movement. For instance, suppose you were told one day that you have a fine ear and would make a very good musician. A talent like that could open all kinds of doors for you. It could give you joy and a purpose, bringing you other people's respect and appreciation.

Then, just for the joy of being good at your music, you would let go of some other things that had been important to you before. You might quit watching a lot of television, for instance, or lose some early morning sleep so that you could practice. You might lose interest in some friends who were once important to you, and gain some new friends who shared your interest. You might even start skimming over other homework to make more time for practicing and listening to music.

Sometimes these sacrifices would be easy. You'd make them without thinking, without ever realizing they were sacrifices. Other times, the sacrifices might be difficult. But as long as the joy of music was close, you'd keep on letting go of other things, clearing them away, to get at it.

If you've gone out for a sport, played in a band, tried to be a good student, or wanted to excel at something else, you know how it works. You keep clearing away what is less important to get at what is most important to you.

This is a picture of the first side of the movement called *repentance*. When Jesus started preaching, he called for repentance in no uncertain terms. But he didn't just say "Repent!" and then turn away, trying to make us feel rotten about ourselves so that we'd try harder. That would be the old self's merry-go-round again. Soon we'd be proud of being ashamed of ourselves. That wouldn't be repentance at all.

No, Jesus announced the gift and stayed with it. "The time is fulfilled, and the kingdom of God has come near," he said. "Repent, and believe in the good news" (Mark 1:15). First he proclaimed the gift, the surprising good news that God is coming to make us and the whole creation new. Then he talked about repentance, calling people to let go of other things they'd clung to in his place.

Jesus did the same with tax collectors and prostitutes. He sat down with them, speaking the Word to them, making his presence felt. And then, like Zaccheus, for the joy of the gift, they repented (Luke 19:1-10).

Jesus does the same with us in our Baptism. Most of us were baptized as infants, before we even knew there was such a thing. That's how the God of the promise works, by coming straight out with it, promising to give us all the gifts of grace, to forgive us, destroy the grave for us, and make us and the whole creation new.

Then comes the repentance, not because we must impress Jesus with how penitent we are, but just because his gifts are so great. Like the hidden treasure, the gifts are buried in a simple ceremony of water and words. But as we receive them, we find out how great and precious these gifts are. And then repentance is set in motion. Like the man who found a treasure hidden in a field, or like you when you've suddenly discovered you're really good at something, we say, "Sell the rest—let everything else take second place. I want this."

There's some sorrow in it, alright, the sorrow of recognizing how in our attempts to impress God we ignore the promise, the sorrow of realizing how we've harmed our neighbors and ourselves. And there's the sorrow of making sacrifices, letting go of some things that have been important. But it's not the pat-me-on-the-back-because-I've-been-so-sincerely-sorry kind of sorrow. It's the sorrow in the midst of joy that comes when we let go of some things that used to be important because now what's really important has come.

That's how the old sinner in us dies. God kills the old you each day with kindness. The God of grace keeps showering you with promises and gifts until finally the old you just plain dies of it. It happens as the Spirit working through the Word enables you to say, "I don't have to impress God anymore or prove that I can take care of myself. I can count on God to keep the word. I repent—you are the Lord. Do what you think is best."

The rising

That's the first side of the movement called repentance—the letting go. Once that's started, the other side follows—taking hold of the gift. "Sell everything," the man in the parable said, "so I can buy that field." "Let everything else go," someone who wants to be good at something says, "I want to do this"—to be a good musician, a good student, a good mechanic, or something else.

Dan Lefebvre

170

As this happens, as the gift takes hold of you, your whole way of looking at things changes. Again, take music for an example. If you didn't think you had a talent for it or didn't enjoy it, you might think that music teachers were fussy and unreasonable, that music students were strange, that the music taught in school or by piano teachers was pretty dull.

But if you found out that you really had a talent for it, all of that would change. Then you'd be all ears for your music teacher, taking in every word in hopes of improving. The other music students would become your companions, people you help and who help you. And music itself, all kinds of music, would take on new excitement.

Everything turns around

That's what happens on the second side of repentance, too. Once God's gifts and promises take hold of you, your whole way of looking at things turns around, so that as Paul says, you "walk in newness of life."

Then God is no longer a glorified fire extinguisher that hangs on the wall for emergencies only. God is your God, the God who has decided for you, the one to whom you turn at all times. Then instead of wondering why your neighbors are so strange, trying to impress them or go them one better, you begin to see the people in your church and other people as friends, people who hear the Word with you, people to be loved and cared for, people who love and care for you.

And then, instead of seeing your life as just one day after another when you have to try to grab the future, you can begin to see your life in terms of God's purposes for you—to serve God, to love your neighbors, to care for the earth. This is the new self that arises, the new you born in the water and Word of Baptism.

All of this doesn't happen automatically, though. For one thing, the sinful self doesn't just drop dead and never return. Though Baptism is its death, it doesn't finally die until you do. And in the meantime, it rages, struggles, fights, quivers, shakes, and rattles as viciously and dangerously as a dying lion, trying to recover.

For another thing, this world isn't the kingdom yet. The new creation has begun in Christ, but he has not yet destroyed all his enemies. As long as death remains, as long as the world wants to go its own way, you are going to have plenty of problems and struggles. And then there's the devil, God's mimic, always ready to fan your questions and doubts into a flame with more doubts and false promises.

That's why Baptism means a *daily* dying and rising, a daily drowning of the old self and a daily rising of the new you in you. Repenting and believing aren't habits—things that we acquire or have installed in us like the automatic pilots on planes. We don't just automatically forget about the other things that have been important to us. And we don't just automatically believe, either.

Then how does it happen? It happens day by day, as God sends the Spirit to speak to us through the Word and to renew us in the sacraments.

"Remember your Baptism," the Spirit says. "As the old self fights and struggles, remember what God did when you were baptized—how God promised to make you one of his own, to make you new and to bring you into his new creation."

"This is my Word," the Spirit says as your pastor and others bear witness to Christ for you. "You are mine and all the gifts are yours." "This is the Lord's Supper," the Spirit says. "In it Christ is with you to open up the future to you."

In these ways, through the Word and the sacraments given in the church, the Spirit will give you faith day by day and keep you in it. The Spirit will set the wheels of repentance in motion in you, prying you away from whatever tries to take its place, wrapping you up in the promise. God sent his Spirit to you in your Baptism to do just that, to kill the old you in you, to raise up the new you day by day, to keep you and make you what you will be. You can be sure of it. God keeps his word. It's for certain.

26
MORE THAN A MEMORY

What is Holy Communion?

Holy Communion is the body and blood of our Lord Jesus Christ given with bread and wine, instituted by Christ himself for us to eat and drink.

Where do the Scriptures say this?

Matthew, Mark, Luke, and Paul say: In the night in which he was betrayed, our Lord Jesus took bread, and gave thanks; broke it, and gave it to his disciples, saying: Take and eat; this is my body, given for you. Do this for the remembrance of me. Again, after supper, he took the cup, gave thanks, and gave it for all to drink, saying: This cup is the new covenant [testament] in my blood, shed for you and for all people for the forgiveness of sin. Do this for the remembrance of me.

Waiting can be both delicious and a torture. It's delicious when something you really want is just around the corner. Then, whether it's as great as summer or as routine as supper, you've got something to look forward to.

But it can be torturous, too. Somehow the clock always seems to slow down during waiting times. And while you wait, there can be all kinds of questions and worries about whether what you're waiting for is ever going to arrive.

That's the kind of situation we're in now as God's people. God has made the decision for us, and through Baptism and the Word given us the gifts of grace. But the new day hasn't come yet. We are waiting, between the times—the time of God's promise and the time of the new day. We have the delicious hope of what is to come. But it is still a hope, and the waiting can be tortured by all kinds of questions and fears.

Christ isn't going to leave us standing, though. While he gives us his gifts, he keeps us surrounded with other believers to wait and hope with us. But he goes further, much further. Besides giving us all the gifts of Baptism and speaking to us in the Word, he gives us the Sacrament of the Altar: the Lord's Supper. In it, he himself comes to be with us in our between times to renew us in his gifts, to unite us as his people in the church, and to give us a taste of the new day.

That's what is most important about this sacrament: Christ's presence with us as we eat and drink the bread and wine with one another.

Eating and drinking

The Lord's Supper goes by many different names, each one emphasizing some part of it. It is called Holy Communion because in it we have union with Christ and other Christians as we eat and drink. Christ participates with us and we who are baptized children participate with him and one another in his gifts (1 Corinthians 10:16). It is also called the Sacrament of the Altar, because we gather around the altar to receive it, and the Eucharist, from a Greek word meaning "thanksgiving," because of the thanks and joy that go with Christ's gifts.

The best name for this sacrament, though, is the one used in the New Testament: the Lord's Supper (1 Corinthians 11:20). It sums up in two words the most important ingredients of the sacrament.

First of all, it is the *Lord's* Supper. Christ instituted the sacrament at the last supper he ate with his disciples, commanding them, and us, to eat the bread and drink the wine in remembrance of him. Christ has the action in the sacrament. It is his

174

Jean-Claude Lejeune

presence with us as we eat and drink, his giving himself to us with the bread and the wine, that renews us in his gifts and gives us a foretaste of what is to come.

Second, it is the Lord's *Supper*. As Christ gave bread and wine to his disciples to eat and drink, he gives bread and wine to us with his promise. Though the servings may be small, it is a meal, a supper. Just as Baptism is a washing in the Word, the Lord's Supper is eating and drinking in the Word. But while Baptism happens to only one person at a time, in the Lord's Supper the whole congregation eats and drinks together.

So, again, the two main things that happen in the sacrament are Christ's giving of his promise and the eating and drinking.

But now we run into the same problem we met with the Sacrament of Holy Baptism. When you look at the Lord's Supper, it can look like a dressed up meal. The pastor speaks some words and the people do some eating and drinking. But the words are like our words—words that anyone can speak and understand. And the bread and wine are plain, ordinary bread and wine—the kinds that can be bought in a store.

Christ's presence with us

The difference between this meal and every other meal is that it is the *Lord's* Supper. He takes bread and says, "This is my body." He takes wine and says, "This cup is the new covenant [testament] in my blood." It is this action, his presence with us, that makes the difference.

There are different ways of trying to understand how Christ is present with us in his supper. Some Christians have argued that Christ is only present in our memories, that since he is divine and in heaven, he can't really be down on earth with us in the eating and drinking. As they see it, the sacrament is a dramatic way of remembering what Christ once did for us.

Other Christians have argued that Christ becomes present with us in his supper by changing the bread and wine into his actual body and blood. This understanding is called *transubstantiation*, or "changing substance." While the bread and wine still look like bread and wine, to this way of thinking their substance changes to become the body and blood.

The differences between these two understandings and the Lutheran understanding of the Lord's Supper are hidden in three small words in Luther's explanation: "Holy Communion *is* the body and blood of our Lord Jesus Christ *given with* bread and wine."

Dale D. Gehman

176

"Holy Communion *is* the body and blood of our Lord Jesus Christ." That little *is* says that Christ is more than a memory—that he is actually present with us as we eat and drink the bread and wine together. This is the heart of the gospel. When he first gave this supper to his disciples, Jesus said, "This *is* my body, given for you." This makes all the difference. It means that the Lord's Supper isn't something we do for Jesus, getting together to have a meal in his memory. Rather, it is something Jesus does for us. He is risen from the dead; he is reigning right now as Lord of the future. He's not tied to some faraway place in the heavens. He can go where he wants and do what he wants. And he wants to be with us.

But now those other little words come along. "Holy Communion is the body and blood of our Lord Jesus Christ *given with* bread and wine." The bread and wine don't change, in substance or in any other way, not any more than the water of Baptism changes. They remain common, ordinary bread and wine. But Christ's body and blood are *given with* them, or, as Luther also said, "in, with, and under the bread and wine."

Do you suppose that our God, who is always giving, would leave us stuck in the middle of our waiting time? The old self would like to think so. It would like to make it seem that God is faraway and never has the time or the interest to bother with the likes of us. And the old Adam or Eve would also like to make it seem that water, bread, and wine are too weak, common, and ordinary for God's uses.

But that's not the way God works. God is always with us; God never leaves us alone. The God who raised Jesus from the dead is always giving and doesn't hold back.

Why this sacrament, then? If God is always with us, if God is always giving, why bother to give us the Sacrament of the Lord's Supper?

God gives it for you, for each of us, for our between times. As long as we're waiting, we're in jeopardy. And as long as we're in jeopardy, God wants to care for us in a way we can't miss. God wants to be sure that we're sure, to be certain we can be certain of the promise. So, in the Lord's Supper, Christ gives us his body and blood with the bread and wine. He takes common, ordinary earthly things and uses them to give himself completely. "Here I am," he says, "given for you."

In this way, Christ picks up and makes us new again. He reassures us that his word of forgiveness is meant precisely for each of us, putting his promise between our teeth so that we can chew it, pouring it out on our lips so that we can taste it, roll it around in our mouths, and swallow it. "This is my body, given for you," he says. "Now you have me. I am yours and you are mine."

In this way, Christ unites us as his people, too. His promise is given with the bread and wine to each of us as the Spirit gathers us together in the communion of the church. In Christ, your friends and neighbors who eat and drink the Lord's Supper with you become your brothers and sisters.

And in this way, Christ gives us a taste of what the end is going to be. "This is what it's going to be like," he says. "We're all going to be together, one big happy family."

That's what makes the Lord's Supper such a great and precious gift. It's not some pious invention designed to give us a dramatic way of remembering Jesus. It is his supper, his gift to us. It is "instituted by Christ himself for us to eat and drink."

"Do this," Jesus said, "Do this for the remembrance of me." With this command, he lets us know that he wants to be with us while we wait. He is more than a memory; he is our Lord. With his command, we can be certain—certain that he's with us from beginning to end, now and always.

27
OPENING THE FUTURE

What benefits do we receive from this sacrament?

The benefits of this sacrament are pointed out by the words, *given and shed for you for the remission of sin.* These words assure us that in the sacrament we receive forgiveness of sins, life, and salvation. For where there is forgiveness of sins, there is also life and salvation.

How can eating and drinking do all this?

It is not eating and drinking that does this, but the words, *given and shed for you for the remission of sins.* These words, along with eating and drinking, are the main thing in the sacrament. And whoever believes these words has exactly what they say, forgiveness of sins.

When Christ forgives, he swings his gift like a double-edged axe. With one edge, he swings back to clear away all the brush and barriers that can tangle and block up our between times. With the other, he swings forward to clear the way to the future. Forgiveness packs all the power of God's promise. It is God's barrier-breaking, future-opening gift.

"For where there is forgiveness of sins," as Luther's explanation says, "there is also life and salvation." It is next best to being raised from the dead.

Clearing the way

If you've ever been part of a family quarrel or had a skirmish with someone at school, you already have some idea of what forgiveness, or the lack of it, can do.

No matter how small or simple, quarrels set up barriers between people. Take a fight between friends, for instance. As long as friends get along, they can enjoy each other and be themselves without worrying when they are together. But when a quarrel gets started, all of that changes. The good times are replaced by hurt feelings, suspicion, dislike, and maybe some fear. The friendship gets blocked off.

These barriers close off the future, too. As long as friends enjoy each other, they look forward to chances to do things together. But when a quarrel breaks out, the future they looked forward to together is lost. They start avoiding one another.

A quarrel like this can become another one of the old you's merry-go-rounds. When one friend, accidentally or intentionally, hurts another, the friend who gets hurt will often repay the hurt in kind. Soon there can be revenge for the revenge and then maybe revenge for revenge for revenge, a full circle.

This doesn't only happen in quarrels, though. All kinds of things can make barriers between people. Even if it is as small as not liking the way someone looks, the dislike blocks a friendship. People who dislike you try to have as little to do with you as possible. Then you don't have any future with them. If you return the dislike, the circle is completed.

One way to stop merry-go-rounds like these is to declare a cease-fire. Quarreling friends, for instance, will sometimes just give up on each other. They stop fighting, but they don't heal the wounds. Leaving the barriers in place, they go their separate ways, former friends who don't fight anymore but don't have anything to do with each other, either.

The only other way to break the circle is through forgiveness. It doesn't just stop the circle; forgiveness breaks it up entirely, clearing away the barriers and opening up the future again.

It's usually not easy. When you ask someone to forgive you, you admit a fault on your part. You're admitting, too, that you really want and need that person for a friend. It can be just as hard when someone asks you for forgiveness. If you do forgive such a person, you're admitting that you want and need the friendship, too.

But when forgiveness happens, everything opens up again. It is a new beginning. All that has stood between you and the other person is cleared away, and you have a future with that person again.

The same thing happens when people accept you the way you are, overlooking things that might make you unattractive. When you are accepted, the barriers are broken and the future is opened—you can make friends and look forward to good times with people who take you the way you are.

That is how forgiveness works: It breaks down barriers and opens up the future.

One of the barriers that can come between God and us is our own guilt. It starts, like a quarrel, with something we do or fail to do—something we do that is obviously wrong or something we fail to do that clearly should have been done. And then it accelerates into the conviction that God is going to condemn us, that there's no hope—even in God's decision for us.

Shame is another barrier. If guilt makes us feel bad about something we've done, shame makes us feel bad about who we are. We become so bad in our own eyes that we can't believe God would ever deal with the likes of us.

But there are many other barriers, as well. Even our little worries can block the way. When the old you is worried, God seems far away. Then you either get so caught up in all you have to do each day that God doesn't seem to matter, or else you become convinced that God wouldn't help you even if God could.

But "where there is forgiveness of sins, there is also life and salvation." When God speaks the Word of forgiveness to you, when Christ gives you the gift of forgiveness in the Supper, God takes the axe to those barriers and shatters and splinters them into a million pieces.

"This is my body," he says, "given for you." "This cup is the new covenant [testament] in my blood, shed for you and for all people for the forgiveness of sin." It is as if Christ says, "Here I am, right here, with you. All of your guilt is destroyed. Everything that you've done and failed to do is wiped out. I accept you, without condition."

The old Adam or Eve dies on these words. When it tries to insist that God is too big and faraway to ever be interested in all that you have to worry about, Christ says, "This is my body, given for you—I am with you and for you." When the old self says, "I have to prove to God that I am religious and deserving, that I'm not so bad after all," Christ replies, "This is my blood, shed for you. You don't have to prove anything. I'm giving myself to you completely."

With the barriers destroyed, the future opens up to you. Forgiveness packs a new future within itself. When Christ says, "This is my body and blood given and shed for you," he is giving himself to us so that we can count on him for the future. Receiving his gifts, we can expect him to care for us and open the way to the new day he has promised.

182

His blood is "shed for you and for all people," for you and for all who commune with you, whether in your congregation or in others throughout the world. In the Lord's Supper, Christ unites you with all of his people in the church so that you can look forward to the future in the company of his saints, caring for them and being cared for by them while you await the new day.

Receiving the gift

But there's one more question: How can eating and drinking bread and wine knock down barriers and open up the future?

If you remember the explanation of Baptism, you already know the answer. The Lord's Supper isn't eating and drinking alone any more than Baptism is water alone. It is eating and drinking in the Word, and it's through the Word that all the gifts come.

"Given and shed for you," Christ says. *For you.* Hearing these words as you eat the bread and drink the wine, you can be certain that all of Christ's gifts are meant for you.

That's how Christ, in the Spirit, renews the new you, giving you faith. When you hear the words "your sins are forgiven," you can be sure that Christ is at work clearing away every obstacle to open up the future. And when you hear the words, "given and shed for you for the forgiveness of sins," you can be certain that Christ is right there with you, *for you*, to do just that. The certainty he gives is faith, "the assurance of things hoped for," as Hebrews calls it (11:1), the confidence that Christ's gifts and promises are meant for you.

Christ has seen to it that forgiveness is proclaimed and given to you over and over again. In this way, he brings us back to our Baptism, renewing us and starting us afresh. And as he forgives, he opens the way to the new day, so that we can look forward to tomorrow and the next day with certainty and hope. That's what forgiveness does: It is Christ's barrier-breaking, future-opening gift, his down payment on the resurrection.

28
TWO TRAPS

When is a person rightly prepared to receive this sacrament?

Fasting and other outward preparations serve a good purpose. However, that person is well prepared and worthy who believes these words, *given and shed for you for the remission of sins.* But anyone who does not believe these words, or doubts them, is neither prepared nor worthy, for the words *for you* require simply a believing heart.

There are a couple of old traps set around the Lord's Supper. But their teeth are still razor sharp, and when they spring, they keep us from the joy of our between times.

The first trap is the idea that we have to do something in order to make the sacrament work. The second is the idea that the sacrament works no matter what we do. In the first, Christ's promise is made into a law; in the second, it's taken for magic.

Do you recognize the traps? They're just two different versions of the same trick that the old sinner in us always uses to undermine God's promise. We've seen them in every section of the Catechism.

There are good reasons for taking a hard look at these traps again, though. For one thing, when the old you springs them, the comfort and joy of the Lord's Supper is destroyed. For another, the old Adam is going to keep setting and resetting them, varying and trying to spring them again, as long as you live.

We'll look at how these traps work and what they do, first of all. Then we'll see how we can expect Christ to keep his promise in his Supper, coming to be with us to free us in our between times.

Rick Whitmer

Who's in charge here?

The key to recognizing both of these traps is to notice the way the old you tries to take charge of the sacrament. That's one of the old sinner's trademarks—wanting to be in control, making what we do so important that what God does doesn't really matter.

Though they may look different, that's the purpose of both of these traps. They reverse things so that the old self, the old you in us, has the action while God sits by. The question to ask, then, is "Who's in charge here? Whose supper is it?"

The first trap, the idea that we have to do something to make the sacrament work, is the religious one. It has dozens of variations.

Sometimes the old self will come on full of sham holiness, talking about what a great gift the Lord's Supper is. "What bothers me, though," it will say, "is how many people take it so lightly and insincerely." Other times, the old you will reverse its approach and talk about how religious and wonderful people can be without bothering with silly things like bread and wine. Or sometimes the old sinner in us will attack the pastor and those who administer the sacrament, saying that they're so irreligious and sinful that God could never give gifts where they're involved.

It's at this point—after making some complaint about the others who receive the Supper, the way it's given, or who gives it—that the old you closes the trap, suggesting that you really have to do something to fix up the sacraments. "If you're going to get what God has to give," it says, "you have to put yourself on the line. You have to prove to God that you're sincere, that you're trying hard, that you really don't want to do wrong anymore."

Now the fact that the old self is playing judge on you or other people who give or receive the Lord's Supper is a sure sign that it's up to no good. Holding court, without being elected or called to do so, is one of the old self's favorite games.

But there's a more serious problem. When the old you gets by with this ploy, everything turns upside down so that what we do with the Lord's Supper matters as much as or more than what Christ does.

Though the old self would never want to come right out and say so, what the complaints and price tags really mean is this: "Christ doesn't know how to give his gifts. I have to help him somehow." Or "Christ doesn't really know whom he's giving these gifts to. These other people aren't nearly as worthy as I am." Or "Christ doesn't know who is helping him give these gifts. I am so much better than they are."

Do you see what this does to the Lord's Supper? It treats Christ as a liar, taking him for someone so incompetent that he doesn't know what he's doing. It makes Communion into something we have to do in order to impress Jesus or somehow win his favor.

And it puts us right back onto the old you's merry-go-round again. Pretty soon we're so worried about how we look, act, and feel when we go to the Supper that there's no comfort or joy in it at all. It's no wonder some people go to the Lord's table looking as though they are facing inoculation. The trap has sprung.

The second trap

The other trap isn't as pious looking. But it's really the other side of the same coin. In this one, the old self says that the sacrament works no matter what we do.

Now again, this trap has all kinds of variations. Sometimes the old sinner in us will try to spring it very religiously. It will start out with all kinds of praise for the sacrament, talking about how wonderful it is that God takes hold and gives us all these gifts. But then, like the Corinthians (1 Corinthians 11:20-21), it will say that since God does so much, it doesn't really matter what we do.

Another favorite variation of this trick works the same on both Baptism and the Lord's Supper. Here the sacraments become something you do so that you'll be immune from whatever evil you may get caught in. It's like a smallpox vaccination; you get baptized or go to Communion once in a while and then you can do whatever you want to. Nothing really matters once the sacraments have been done to you.

The warning to this trap is the same as it is in the first one. No matter how much it talks about how good and great God's gifts are, the old Adam or Eve retains its grip on the action. What God does in the sacraments has to take a backseat to whatever the old you wants to get away with.

What happens to the sacrament then? It becomes a ticket the old self uses to get whatever it wants, a license it shows when it is questioned or in trouble. Holy Communion is treated like a no-fault insurance policy, picked up at bargain rates every few months or so just in case the old you has an accident.

You can see, then, how both of these traps turn things around so that the old you has the action. In the first one, the old self figures that it has to help God with God's work. In the second, it figures that God is supposed to help it with the old self's work. Either way, if you ask, "Who's in charge here?" the old you's answer is "Me! I'm in charge." The old self sits in the driver's seat while God is supposed to hitchhike or slump in the backseat, being carried along.

How are we going to find our way between these traps? Take another look at that question, "Who's in charge here?" Who is in charge? Who instituted the sacrament of the Lord's Supper? Who said, "This is my body. . . . This is my blood . . . given and shed for you for the forgiveness of sins"? Who said, "Do this for the remembrance of me"?

That's the answer. As long as we try to take over the action, even if it's just trying to find our own way through the traps, we wind up going in circles. The old you has us on the merry-go-round again.

But when the Lord's Supper is recognized for what it is— the Lord's Supper, Christ's gift to us—all of that changes.

What do you do when you know you're going to receive a great gift? You don't do much of anything, do you? You wait for it, you look forward to the gift, you get ready to receive it.

Jean-Claude Lejeune

189

But you certainly don't run around talking about what you've done to deserve the gift, do you? Nor do you set out to try to earn the gift somehow, not if it's really a gift.

And when you're given the gift, what do you do with it? Nobody has to stand over you saying, "Now you have to accept this. You'd better take this gift and look after it." If the gift were of little value, somebody might have to say that to you. But if it's a good gift, something you've wanted, you don't have to be told to do anything. You take the gift and open the wrapping as fast as you politely can. And then you thank the person who gave it to you and enjoy the gift you've received.

CLEO Freelance Photo

That's how the Lord's Supper is to be received. It is a sheer, absolute gift in which Christ lays himself open to us, filling us with his grace.

Because it's a gift, there is nothing you have to do to receive it. But because the Lord's Supper is such a great gift, there might be some things you *want* to do just to get ready for it. You might want to fast, for instance, going without food the morning before the sacrament, just to remind yourself that

Jean-Claude Lejeune

the bread and wine are Christ's gifts. Or you might want to prepare in some other way.

Such preparations "serve a good purpose," as Luther says. But they aren't something we have to do; rather they are some things that we may want to do just because the gift is so great.

The same applies to believing God's promise in the sacrament. If it were something that we had to do "by our own understanding or effort," it would be a chore. Then we would either worry about whether we believe well enough or end up saying that it doesn't matter.

But when the Lord's Supper is recognized as a gift, we can look forward to it eagerly. Then we can expect Christ to give us the faith to believe the Word, to keep his promise to be present with us. And we can expect him to give us all that goes with his presence. That is believing: expecting the promise, expecting Christ to give you his gifts, counting on him to keep his word.

This is why Christ instituted the Lord's Supper in the first place: to renew you in faith, to break down the barriers that separate you from God and your neighbors, and to open up the future to you. Jesus doesn't require you to believe and then leave you squirming, trying to come up with enough believing. He calls you to faith and then gives it to you, sending the Spirit to speak to you through the Word and uphold and uplift you in his sacraments. The Spirit was sent to you in your Baptism, and it will be with you until the last day to do just that: to give you faith and keep you in it.

That's why the Lord's Supper can also be called the Eucharist, "the thanksgiving." It is Christ's gift to us, a means Jesus uses to assure us that he is with us in our between times. So it is full of joy and thanksgiving, packed full and overflowing with Christ's greatest gift to us: himself. As long as he keeps giving, "[nothing] will be able to separate us from the love of God in Christ Jesus our Lord" (Romans 8:39). That's for certain—it is God's Word.

29
KEY TO THE KINGDOM

THE OFFICE OF THE KEYS

What is the "Office of the Keys"?

It is that authority which Christ gave to his church to forgive the sins of those who repent and to declare to those who do not repent that their sins are not forgiven.

What are the words of Christ?

Our Lord Jesus Christ said to his disciples: "Receive the Holy Spirit. If you forgive the sins of any, they are forgiven; if you retain the sins of any, they are retained" (John 20:23).

"Truly, I say to you, whatever you bind on earth shall be bound in heaven, and whatever you loose on earth shall be loosed in heaven" (Matthew 18:18).

CONFESSION

What is private confession?

Private confession has two parts. First, we make a personal confession of sins to the pastor, and then we receive absolution, which means forgiveness as from God himself. This absolution we should not doubt, but firmly believe that thereby our sins are forgiven before God in heaven.

What sins should we confess?

Before God we should confess that we are guilty of all sins, even those which are not known to us, as we do in the Lord's Prayer. But in private confession, as before the pastor, we should confess only those sins which trouble us in heart and mind.

What are such sins?

We can examine our everyday life according to the Ten Commandments—for example, how we act toward father or mother, son or daughter, husband or wife, or toward the people with whom we work, and so on. We may ask ourselves whether we have been disobedient or unfaithful, bad-tempered or dishonest, or whether we have hurt anyone by word or deed.

How might we confess our sins privately?

We may say that we wish to confess our sins and to receive absolution in God's name. We may begin by saying, "I, a poor sinner, confess before God that I am guilty of many sins." Then we should name the sins that trouble us. We may close the confession with the words, "I repent of all these sins and pray for mercy. I promise to do better with God's help."

What if we are not troubled by any special sins?

We should not torture ourselves with imaginary sins. If we cannot think of any sins to confess (which would hardly ever happen), we need not name any in particular, but may receive absolution because we have already made a general confession to God.

How may we be assured of forgiveness?

The pastor may pronounce the absolution by saying, "By the authority of our Lord Jesus Christ I forgive you your sins in the name of the Father and of the Son and of the Holy Spirit. Amen."

Those who are heavily burdened in conscience the pastor may comfort and encourage with further assurances from God's Word.

Skjold

These two explanations might look strangely out of place in the Catechism. To many people, both the keys and private confession don't seem Lutheran. But Christ gave the Office of the Keys to his whole church, and even if you don't recognize the name, it is practiced each Sunday in your congregation.

Private confession isn't practiced as much as it should be among Lutherans, but it, too, is a part of our heritage. For many centuries, it was a regular part of Lutheran church life.

The keys

The Office of the Keys gets its name from a passage that isn't quoted in the Catechism but says virtually the same thing as what is quoted: Matthew 16:19. "I will give you the keys of the kingdom of heaven," Jesus said to Peter and the other disciples, "and whatever you bind on earth will be bound in heaven, and whatever you loose on earth will be loosed in heaven."

The key to the kingdom is forgiveness, Christ's barrier-breaking, future-opening gift. Just as a key opens a door that has been locked shut, Christ's gift of forgiveness breaks down all the barriers the old self raises between us and the gospel.

And just as a key opens a door so that you can be taken into a house, Christ's gift of forgiveness opens up the future so that he can take you into it. With this gift, Christ opens up all his gifts to you, promising to make you and the whole creation new.

Jean-Claude Lejeune

Now Jesus wants to make sure that the key gets used and used properly. So he created an office to look after the key, to see to it that the word of forgiveness is declared to you. "Receive the Holy Spirit," he said to Peter and all the disciples. "If you forgive the sins of any, they are forgiven; if you retain the sins of any, they are retained" (John 20:23).

Because Christ has given this key, we can hear his word of forgiveness spoken to us each Sunday. Following the con-

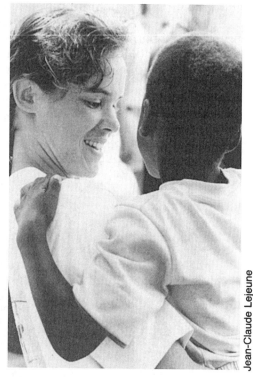

Jean-Claude Lejeune

fession of sin at the beginning of each service, the pastor turns to the congregation and says, "As a called and ordained minister of the Church of Christ, and by his authority, I therefore declare to you the entire forgiveness of all your sins (*LBW*, p. 56)." These words are called the absolution.

As this word is spoken to you, you can be sure God is forgiving you all your sin, that God has and always will. Christ himself is turning the key for you, breaking down your yesterdays and opening up your tomorrows.

Confession

Sometimes, though, the words of absolution spoken on Sunday morning don't strike home the way they should. When they are spoken to the whole congregation, they can leave you wondering if Christ's gift of forgiveness is really meant for you.

In Luther's day, the Roman Catholic church required private confession, insisting that all people had to confess all their sins before they could receive the Lord's Supper. Confession was, and is, one of the sacraments of the Roman Catholic church.

During the Reformation, Luther fought some of these requirements regarding private confession. For one thing, there's no basis in Scripture for demanding that a person confess every sin to a pastor or priest before Communion. But more seriously, when demands like this are made, confession becomes another one of the old self's merry-go-rounds. No matter how much people confess, they can still be left wondering if they've included everything and been completely sincere about it.

But while he fought the requirements in confession, Luther always insisted that confession and absolution is a precious gift. He took away the demand to confess everything, saying that "we should confess only those sins which trouble us in heart and mind." But he strongly urged all Christians to go to private confession and hear the absolution spoken directly to them.

It is hearing the words of the absolution spoken directly and personally to each of us that makes private confession so powerful and helpful.

Jean-Claude Lejeune

Confessing your sins privately with your pastor gives you a chance to get anything that is bothering you off your chest, to talk it over with someone you can trust. Your pastor's job is to help you discover the old self's tricks and traps, to hear you as you confess, and to tell you how God has promised to help you do better.

This alone makes confession a great gift. Often times just being able to talk over what you feel guilty about, are ashamed or afraid of, with someone you can trust will lighten your load.

But there's even more. As the pastor speaks the words of the absolution to you directly, in person, Christ is at work breaking down your barriers and opening up the future to you. "By the command of our Lord Jesus Christ, I . . . forgive you your sins in the name of the Father, and of the Son, and of the Holy Spirit" (*LBW,* p. 197), the pastor can say.

The practice of private confession was discontinued among Lutherans for many different reasons. But the old sinner and the devil are the ones who really stole it, hiding it from us. Though not required, with the Word and the sacraments confession is a means God uses to give us the certainty of faith as we look forward to the dawning of the new day.

30
CONVERSATION AND CONSOLATION

We shall now return to the Gospel, which offers counsel and help against sin in more than one way, for God is surpassingly rich in his grace: First, through the spoken word, by which the forgiveness of sin (the peculiar function of the Gospel) is preached to the whole world; second, through Baptism; third, through the holy Sacrament of the Altar; fourth, through the power of keys; and finally, through the mutual conversation and consolation of the brethren. Matthew 18:20, "Where two or three are gathered," etc.

Smalcald Articles Part III, Article IV

God's grace comes to us in one other way that is often overlooked, one that you've probably seen in operation and drawn strength and encouragement from. In fact, it's probably one of the most important things that has happened for you in your congregation.

Luther called it "the mutual conversation and consolation of the brethren." It is the friendship or fellowship you share with others around you who belong to Christ, another powerful means God uses to keep us in grace.

Your priesthood

The clues to how this "mutual conversation and consolation" becomes an avenue of God's grace are in the Third Article of the Creed and the Sacrament of Baptism.

The Spirit loves company. As the Spirit of Christ goes to work in the Word and the sacraments to give us the certainty of faith, it is always gathering us together with other people—whether in twos and threes, tens and twelves, or hundreds and thousands. The company of others in your congregation isn't an accident. As a member of the church, you are part of the "communion of saints," the community of people put together by the Spirit.

Jean-Claude Lejeune

The Spirit goes further. In Baptism, as God declares the Word for us, the Spirit makes each one of us a special kind of priest. The Spirit calls out the new you in us so that we can speak the word to others, so that we can comfort and help one another along the way.

That may sound like a strange way to put it. You probably don't think of yourself as a priest. But God likes to talk, especially to you and those around you. So God makes each of you a speaker of the Word, a priest, surrounding you with a "priesthood of believers." When you were baptized, you became such a priest.

Your pastor, the one who preaches on Sunday, was called by God and elected by your congregation to hold a special office. In that office, your pastor's calling is to see to it that the Word is properly preached and the sacraments administered.

But your pastor doesn't replace you. Though you might never enter a pulpit, baptize a child, or give the Lord's Supper, as one of God's people you are part of the priesthood. No matter where you go, no matter what kind of job you wind up doing for a living, you can speak the Word of God to others. You can comfort and console, help and encourage others in your congregation. Others can do the same for you.

One of the best examples of how this ministry happens takes place when someone from your church dies. Then people from your congregation gather around the family to comfort them, to say the word of love and hope, to help out in many different ways. It's not always easy, but in this way grieving families are strengthened and upheld in difficult times. This is "the mutual conversation and consolation of the brethren," the kind of help the Spirit gives us as we are gathered together with others.

But it doesn't only happen at a time of death. It goes on all your life long. The comments you've made and the questions you've asked as you've studied the Catechism, for instance, may have helped others gain a deeper understanding. Getting together to have a program and some fun at church youth groups may have opened the door to some new friends. It's this giving and taking, this talking and listening, that the Spirit uses to help each of us. It is a ministry that we have to one another in our churches.

Your gifts

This ministry we have together doesn't only happen in conversation. As Paul describes the church in Romans 12 and 1 Corinthians 12–14, he speaks of a whole variety of gifts the Spirit gives us so that we can serve in other ways, too.

The Holy Spirit doesn't have an assembly line that turns out everyone the same. The Spirit loves variety, making us all different, giving each of us particular gifts. Some of the gifts Paul mentions are preaching, serving, teaching, encouraging, contributing, giving aid, acting mercifully, helping, healing, and even organizing meetings. Along with these gifts are others like prophecy and speaking in tongues.

Having given us our gifts, the Spirit takes us and binds us together in our congregations to pool these gifts. The Holy Spirit unites us as God's people, making us a community, so that we can each give from our strengths to make good each other's weaknesses. We are made one body, as Paul says, the body of Christ. Just as hands, feet, arms, and legs serve different purposes for the same person, we have different gifts and functions but we are united as one in Christ.

The purpose of our gifts isn't to serve ourselves, though. As the Spirit gives us the Word and the gifts that go with it, we are turned both inward and outward—in toward the people we belong with in the church, and out toward all who have not yet heard the Word or been grasped by it. That's the church's purpose: to speak the Word to all who have ears to hear, to give the gifts we share to any and all who need them.

The old self turns up its nose at these gifts just as it turns up its nose at everything God gives. "The mutual conversation and consolation of the brethren," as the old sinner in us sees it, is just so much talk—people getting together in the church to visit as they do everywhere else. It's just fellowship, something you can do anywhere; or it's all fellowship, that's all the church has to offer.

The old sinner in us does the same thing to the Spirit's gifts. In its eyes, they are just talents, special abilities you're born with so that you can impress people or make lots of money. Or else the old you puts on some religion again and claims that your gifts give you a corner on God's market, insisting that you must be the finest Christian around.

Either way, as the old self takes them, God's gifts are just common, ordinary, natural things to be used in the ordinary way to take care of yourself.

God sees these gifts differently. God loves what's common, ordinary, and natural. God is the one who made all things, all that's great and all that's common, all that's beautiful and all that's ordinary. God is the one who was born in an ordinary stable to become a person like us. God is the one who died a terrifying death and was put away in an ordinary grave. God is the one who raised Jesus from the dead, the one who sends the Spirit to speak to us in ordinary words, to adopt us, to assure us and reassure us that we belong to him by using natural things as common as water, bread, and wine.

It is this God, the God who has made a decision for us in Christ Jesus, who is your God. That's God's decision. That's God's promise—to take you as you are, with all that's great and all that's common about you, with all that's beautiful and all that's ordinary about you, to make you new, one of his very own.

James L. Shaffer

205

God is going to make you what Adam and Eve were made to be in the first place. God is making you a believer, one with ears for the Word just because it is God's Word. God is going to make you a lover, one who will give your gifts to your neighbors just because they're neighbors. God is going to make you a steward, one who cares for the earth, for all that's common, ordinary and natural, just because it's God's creation.

But that's not all. As God makes you new, God's going to make the whole creation new, bringing in the new heavens and the new earth. Then the old you, death, and the devil will be gone, washed up once and for all. Then God will dwell with us, as loving fathers and mothers live with their children.

In the meantime, God gives us all that we need: the Word, the sacraments, and the company of others. They are God's gifts, given in the Spirit to make us new each day, to hold and keep us until the new day comes. It's for certain. It's God's promise. God has decided. God keeps his word.

DAILY PRAYERS

MORNING PRAYER

In the morning, when you rise, make the sign of the cross and say, "In the name of God, the Father, the Son, and the Holy Spirit. Amen."

Then, kneeling or standing, say the Apostles' Creed and the Lord's Prayer. Then you may say this prayer:

I give thanks to you, heavenly Father, through Jesus Christ your dear Son, that you have protected me through the night from all danger and harm. I ask you to preserve and keep me, this day also, from all sin and evil, that in all my thoughts, words, and deeds I may serve and please you. Into your hands I commend my body and soul and all that is mine. Let your holy angels have charge of me, that the wicked one have no power over me. (Adapted from Responsive Prayer 1, *LBW*, p. 163.)

After singing a hymn (possibly a hymn on the Ten Commandments) or whatever your devotion may suggest, you should go to your work joyfully.

EVENING PRAYER

In the evening, when you retire, make the sign of the cross and say, "In the name of God, the Father, the Son, and the Holy Spirit. Amen."
Then, kneeling or standing, say the Apostles' Creed and the Lord's Prayer. Then you may say this prayer:

I give thanks to you, heavenly Father, through Jesus Christ your dear Son, that you have this day so graciously protected me. I beg you to forgive me all my sins and the wrong which I have done. By your great mercy defend me from all the perils and dangers of this night. Into your hands I commend my body and soul, and all that is mine. Let your holy angels have charge of me, that the wicked one have no power over me. (Adapted from Responsive Prayer 2, *LBW*, p. 166.)

These prayers were originally included in Luther's Small Catechism.

Jean-Claude Lejeune